Preface

This series, intended for use in college courses and at GCE Advanced level, seeks actively to involve students with historical evidence. Each book provides a wealth of contemporary material for study; this material will not only illustrate many aspects of the period under study, but will also face students with some of the problems which begin to arise whenever original source material is used.

In each book questions are posed which are basic to the period concerned. The documents which follow are intended to be read with the questions in mind, and they will begin to suggest possible answers. Inevitably, they will also confront the reader with many further questions, with apparent contradictions, with problems of bias, of lack of clarity, and of interpretation – in short, with the complexity of historical judgments. The student should thus gain insights into the period under study, into the type of original material available for the study, and into the task of the historian.

This volume deals with selected important themes of British Foreign Policy from the period of Gladstone and Disraeli to the outbreak of the First World War.

S. R. Gibbons
S. J. Houston
General Editors

Contents

C.

BRITISH FOREIGN POLICY 1870–1914

JUDITH TELFORD

EVIDENCE IN
HISTORY

EVIDENCE IN
HISTORY

GENERAL EDITORS:
Stephen R. Gibbons
Head of Combined Studies
College of Sarum St Michael
Salisbury

Stanley J. Houston
Head of History
King's College School
Wimbledon

PUBLISHED BY:
Blackie & Son Limited
Bishopbriggs, Glasgow G64 2NZ
450 Edgware Road, London W2 1EG

PRINTED IN GREAT BRITAIN BY:
Robert MacLehose & Co. Limited, Printers to the University of Glasgow

The Foreign Policy of Gladstone & Disraeli

1

The politics of the 1870s and 1880s are dominated by the rivalry between Gladstone and Disraeli. To a remarkable degree their opposed backgrounds, personalities and style were the focus of politics, seized on alike by voters, by *Punch* cartoonists, and by foreign observers. Their polemics emphasized their personal animosity and highlighted their political differences. Biographies abound in references to the 'profound differences' in their views on almost all subjects, and most notably, on foreign affairs.

At the same time, however, it is possible for many historians to accept Langer's view that 'one of the remarkable things about the history of modern England is the singleness of purpose of all parties in the conduct of foreign affairs. There was a veritable cult of the principle of continuity and it is consequently useless to look for fundamental divergencies on matters of major importance. ... If we consider the broad lines of British policy at the close of the Victorian Era ... we find that there has been surprisingly little change since the days of Napoleon.'[1] Langer's assessment of what constitutes the matters of major importance is also echoed by most historians – preoccupation with the Empire, 'reliance on a strong navy', a tendency to favour a balance of power in Europe and the 'foremost British interest, peace, pursued by all successive foreign secretaries from Pitt to Grey'.

Does an examination of the policies of Gladstone and Disraeli in some key areas of foreign policy support the view that despite the vilification that each heaped on the other, and the apparent polarity of their views, both recognized the same fundamental and continuing guidelines of British policy?

Were there fundamental differences in the foreign policies of Gladstone and Disraeli?

Personal antipathy

Certainly there is ample evidence of the animosity between the two men:

[1] THE DIPLOMACY OF IMPERIALISM *By W. Langer   Knopf, New York, 1951* p.790.

Rarely in our history has there been so complete a contrast between two notable protagonists as that between Disraeli and Gladstone.

Their profound difference in outlook. . .

The questions over which they joined issue stand at the very root of international relations.

All from DISRAELI, GLADSTONE AND THE EASTERN QUESTION
by R. Seton-Watson   Macmillan, 1935

Granville to Queen Victoria, 24 April 1880:

Lord Beaconsfield and Mr Gladstone are men of extraordinary ability; they dislike each other more than is usual among public men.

LETTERS OF QUEEN VICTORIA, *2nd Series III 86*

Henry Loch (Gov. Isle of Man) to Lord Lytton, 21 November 1878. India Office Library:

I have never known such strong feeling to exist on any question as on this [Afghan] and the Turkish Question . . . and it is all purely personal, the divergence of opinion not being so much upon the merits of the question which seems seldom understood, but upon the feelings that are entertained either towards Lord Beaconsfield or Mr Gladstone.

Gladstone to Lord Rendel, Lord Rendel's Personal Papers (1931):

In past times the Tory party had principles by which it would and did stand for bad and for good. All this Dizzy destroyed.

Gladstone to Sir A. Gordon, 16 August 1876, on Disraeli's elevation to the Peerage:

His Government is supposed now to stand mainly upon its recent foreign policy; the most selfish and least worthy I have ever known.

Disraeli, at a banquet, 1878, about Gladstone:

A sophisticated rhetoretician, inebriated with the exuberance of his own verbosity.

Disraeli to Derby, about Gladstone:

Posterity will do justice to that unprincipled maniac Gladstone – extraordinary mixture of envy, vindictiveness, hypocrisy, and superstition.

Attitude to Europe

In *The Foreign Policy of Victorian England* K. Bourne asserts that 'Britain's circumstances dictate a particular attitude towards the continent of Europe. Her special position was her island security. But this only sheltered her from the Continent, it did not isolate her. What she lacked in Europe were aggressive ambitions, not substantial interests. Her empire – formal or informal – did not eliminate or even depreciate the importance of her European connections. Rather it stressed the interdependence of her global and her European policies. Europe remained for the whole of the century one of Britain's biggest markets and the greatest threat to her security.'

Do the letters and speeches of the two statesmen offer evidence that they were aware of a 'particular attitude' governing and making compatible their European policies? Both made major speeches on the subject.

Lord Beaconsfield. Speech at the Guildhall, 9 November 1879:

> One of the greatest of Romans, when asked what were his policies, replied 'Imperium et Libertas'. That would not make a bad programme for a British Ministry. . . . If one of the most extensive and wealthiest empires in the world ... from a perverse interpretation of its insular geographical position, turns an indifferent ear to the feelings and fortunes of Continental Europe, such a course would, I believe, only end in its becoming an object of general plunder. So long as the power and advice of England are felt in the Councils of Europe, peace, I believe, will be maintained and for a long period. Without their presence war ... seems to me inevitable.

Seton-Watson comments on this speech:

> Here in a few phrases Beaconsfield summed up the very essence of British policy reminding us that despite our favoured insular position and our vast interests overseas, we can never neglect Europe, save at our mortal peril, and that a neglect of our commitments and our international responsibility, so far from achieving the idea of 'splendid isolation' would almost infallibly confront us with a hostile continental coalition.
> BRITAIN IN EUROPE, 1789–1914
> *by R. Seton-Watson   Cambridge, 1937*   *p.544*

Disraeli to the House of Commons, 4 July 1864:

> Since the settlement that followed the great revolutionary war, England has on the whole followed a Conservative foreign policy, I mean a foreign policy interested in the tranquillity and prosperity of the world, the normal condition of which is peace. ... The position of England in the Councils of Europe is essentially that of a moderating and mediating Power. Her interest and her policy are, when changes are inevitable and necessary, to assist so that these changes, if possible, may be accomplished without war.
> *Hansard Parliamentary Debates   3rd Series   Vol. CLXXVI 1864 Col. 745*

Disraeli. Speech at the Free Trade Hall, Manchester, 3 April 1872:
> Don't suppose, because I counsel firmness and decision at the right moment, that I am of that school of statesmen who are favourable to a turbulent and aggressive diplomacy. I have resisted it during a great part of my life . . . . I acknowledge that the policy of England with respect to Europe should be a policy of reserve, but proud reserve; and in answer to those statesmen, those mistaken statesmen, who have intimated the decay of the power of England and the decline of her resources, I express here my confident conviction that there never was a moment in our history when the power of England was so great and her resources so great and inexhaustible.

Gladstone to General Gray (the Queen's Private Secretary):
> I do not believe that England ever will or can be unfaithful to her great traditions, or can forswear her interest in the common transactions and the general interests of Europe. . . . Do not allow it to be believed that England will never interfere . . . for any reasonable belief in such an abnegation on the part of England, there is no ground whatever . . . she should not encourage the weak by giving expectations of aid to resist the strong, but should rather seek to deter the strong by firm but moderate language from aggression on the weak.

Gladstone on foreign policy to a Liberal deputation, 29 March 1878:
> The Pursuit of Objects which are European, by means which are European, in concert with the mind of the rest of Europe and supported by its Authority . . .

Gladstone. Speech made during the third Midlothian Campaign, 27 November 1879:
> In my opinion the third sound principle (of foreign policy) is this – to strive and cultivate and maintain, ay to the very utmost, what is called the Concert of Europe, to keep the Powers of Europe in union together. And why? Because in keeping all in union together you neutralize and fetter and bind up the selfish aims of each. . . . Common action means common objects, and the only objects for which you can unite together the Powers of Europe are objects connected with the Common Good of them all.

The Belgian Question

Do specific issues of European policy offer any evidence of unanimity of approach? The probability of war between France and Prussia raised the question of Belgian neutrality. Seton-Watson comments that 'in the sixties and during the war of 1870 Stanley, Disraeli, Clarendon, Granville, and Gladstone alike adhered to the principles laid down by

Palmerston in the Belgian question'. Bourne thinks Gladstone's views 'not essentially different from his predecessors'!

Gladstone to the House of Commons, 10 August 1870:
> What is our interest in maintaining the neutrality of Belgium? It is the same as that of every great power in Europe. It is contrary to the interests of Europe that there should be unmeasured aggrandizement ... is there any man who hears me who does not feel that if, in order to satisfy a greedy appetite for aggrandizement, coming whence it may, Belgium was absorbed, the day that witnessed that absorption would hear the knell of public right and public law in Europe?
> *Hansard Parliamentary Debates 3rd Series Vol. CCIII 1870 Col. 1786*

Disraeli, replying for the Opposition:
> I infer from the statement of the right honourable Gentleman that Her Majesty's Government have taken decided steps to maintain and defend the neutrality of Belgium. That will be a satisfactory intimation to the country generally. .... I accept it as a wise and spirited policy, in my opinion, not the less wise because it is spirited. I cannot myself believe that the position of England is such that she can no longer take an interest in the affairs of the Continent of Europe, or attempt to exercise that influence which has been so often exercised not only with advantage to this Country but with great benefit to the Continent itself. .... Viewing it from a very limited point of view, it is of the highest importance to this Country that the whole Coast from Ostend to the North Sea should be in the hands of free and flourishing communities.
> *ibid.*

The Balkans

Perhaps the area where Disraeli and Gladstone appeared to clash most violently was the Balkans. 'The Near East' concerned Britain because of the proximity of Turkey to her sea routes through the Mediterranean. Should she stand aside and allow other Powers, and especially Russia, to break into the Eastern Mediterranean by letting Turkey collapse? Certainly, especially when the 'Bulgarian Atrocities' became known, Gladstone made statements that seemed to suggest that any support for Turkey would be impossible for him.

Gladstone. Speech at Southwark, 21 September 1878:
> We have seen this degrading despotism bursting out at times into a fury of cruelty, savagery, lust, and every imaginable depravity.

Gladstone. Pamphlet 'The Bulgarian Horrors', 9 September 1876:
> The basest and blackest outrages upon record within the present

century, if not within the memory of man. I entreat my countrymen to require and to insist that our Government, which has been working in one direction, shall work in the other. . . . Let the Turks now carry away their abuses in the only possible manner, namely by carrying off themselves. Their Zaptiehs and their Mudirs, their Bimbashis and their Yŭzbashirs, their Kaimakams and their Pashas, one and all, bag and baggage, shall I hope clear out from the province they have desolated and profaned.

Not that Gladstone's Bulgarian policy was noticably different from Salisbury's; as the Russians complained, it was just as bad.

The principal difficulty lay not in identifying the problem but in arriving at any decision to resolve it in view of the violent internal dissension that the project of supporting the Turks aroused. This distaste was not confined to Gladstone or the nonconformist conscience, but was equally marked within the Conservative Cabinet.

THE RELUCTANT IMPERIALISTS, vol. I
by C. Lowe   Routledge & Kegan Paul, 1967   *pp.27 & 22*

In spite of all the noise that Gladstone had made over the Bulgarian horrors, he did not, it would seem, differ so very much even from Disraeli about the substance of British interests in the Near East . . . he knew that the country still believed the strategic security of Constantinople to be a fundamental necessity to British interests . . . therefore 'bag and baggage' was defined as a demand only from Bosnia – for the expulsion of Turkish Officials. Even in Bulgaria Gladstone admitted that he envisaged the Sultan would retain his 'titular sovereignty'.

THE FOREIGN POLICY OF VICTORIAN ENGLAND
by K. Bourne   Clarendon, 1970   *p.137*

Gladstone. Speech at Blackheath, 9 September 1876:
You shall retain your titular sovereignty, your Empire shall not be invaded, but never again as the years roll in their course, so far as it is in our power to determine, never again shall the hand of violence be raised by you, never again shall the floodgates of lust be open to you, never again shall the dire refinements of cruelty be devised to you. . . .

Disraeli to the House of Commons, 11 August 1876:
I agree . . . that even the slightest estimate of the horrors that occurred in Bulgaria is quite sufficient to excite the indignation of the country and of Parliament.
    We are always treated as if we had some peculiar alliance with

the Turkish Government, as if we were their peculiar friends, and even as if we were expected to uphold them in any enormity they might commit. I want to know what evidence there is of that, what interest we have in such a thing. We are, it is true, the Allies of the Sultan of Turkey; so is Russia, so is Austria, so is France. ... We are also their partners in a tripartite Treaty in which we not only generally, but singly guarantee ... the territorial integrity of Turkey ... The Government of the Porte was never for a moment misled by the arrival of the British Fleet in Besika Bay. They were perfectly aware when that Fleet came there, that it was not to prop up any decaying and obsolete Government, nor did its presence there sanction any of those enormities which are the subject of our painful discussion tonight. ... If it should happen that the Government which controls the greater portion of those fair lands is found to be incompetent for its purpose, neither England nor any of the Great Powers will shrink from fulfilling the high political and moral duty which will then devolve upon them. ... what our duty is at this critical moment is to maintain the Empire of England.

We do not uphold Turkey from blind superstition and from a want of sympathy with the highest aspiration of humanity.

Hansard Parliamentary Debates   3rd Series   Vol. CCXXI   1876   Col. 1140

Disraeli to Queen Victoria, 16 May 1876:

They (the Government) from the first, warned the Porte that it must not look to them for assistance. ... At the same time, they think it right that there should be no misunderstanding as to their position and intentions ... The vast importance of Constantinople, whether in a military, a political, or a commercial point of view, is too well understood to require explanation. It is therefore scarcely necessary to point out that Her Majesty's Government are not prepared to witness with indifference the passing into other hands than those of its present possessors, of a capital holding so peculiar and commanding a position.

Commenting on the Treaty of Berlin, which Salisbury and Disraeli regarded at the time as the triumph of their Near Eastern diplomacy, Gladstone said that it contained 'some great results for humanity'.

Gladstone to the House of Commons, 7 May 1877:

That most masterly paper in which Lord Salisbury ... has torn up the Turkish Constitution into rags, and held it up to the contempt and derision of mankind.

Hansard Parliamentary Debates   3rd Series   Vol. CCXXIV   1877   Col. 466

Territorial arrangements made at the Congress of Berlin.

Gladstone to the House of Commons, commenting on Lord Derby's despatch on Bulgarian Atrocities:

> The language of that despatch was as strong as the language used at any of the meetings held last autumn – Lord Derby demanded that the authors of the massacres should be punished.
> *ibid.*

> It appeared to me to be of the utmost importance that there should be, if possible, some union of sentiment upon the subject. I at least wished to do all that was in my power to prevent the question falling into the category of Party questions. ... I have taken the phrase 'practical self government' because I found it in the despatch of Lord Salisbury ... and because substantially it appeared to me to comprise all that was requisite.
> *ibid.*

Continuity of Policy

'Actions speak louder than words'. What happened when the Liberals came back to power in 1880?

In his electoral manifesto, Gladstone had accused his opponents of weakening the Empire 'by needless wars, unprofitable extension, and unwise engagements' and of dishonouring it in the eyes of Europe by 'filching the Island of Cyprus'. ... It was widely assumed in the country that 'a complete reversion in foreign affairs' would follow the Liberal victory. Yet in the speech from the Throne the new Government proclaimed as one of its foremost aims 'the complete and early fulfilment of the Treaty of Berlin' and when the Queen told Granville that she would never 'sanction a reversal of the policy of the last few years' he assured her, that instead of destroying the Berlin Treaty, the Government was 'determined to do their best to carry out its provisions'. Even as regards Cyprus ... he followed this up with the highly disingenuous proposal to keep the island.

BRITAIN IN EUROPE, 1789–1914
by R. Seton-Watson   Cambridge, 1937   *p.548*

The actual difference in British policy towards Asia Minor brought about by the advent of the Liberals in 1880 was, therefore, minimal, a fact which has been obscured by Salisbury's abuse of his successors, and Gladstone's denunciations of the Cyprus Convention. ... Much as he disliked the Turks personally Gladstone fully admitted their necessity to British interests.

THE RELUCTANT IMPERIALISTS, vol. I
by C. Lowe   Routledge & Kegan Paul, 1967   *p.37*

In general the concepts of 1878–82 remained the basis of policy in Europe for the next twenty-five years. Nor was there any great difference when Gladstone took over the reins in 1880. ... It is a basic error to take Gladstone's Midlothian pronouncements as Liberal foreign policy: this, after all, was an election campaign when he had to develop a line antagonistic to that of Disraeli, and his actions, once in office, were very different. Gladstone himself in conversation with Granville in September 1880 recognized 'the expediency of maintaining as far as might be a continuity in Foreign Policy' and certainly he made no attempt to abandon participation for isolation.

THE RELUCTANT IMPERIALISTS, vol. I
by C. Lowe   Routledge & Kegan Paul, 1967   *p.21*

Imperial Policies
Another area in which Disraeli and Gladstone are painted as arch enemies is the Empire. Disraeli, with his exuberance over the purchase of the Canal Shares and the Imperial title for Victoria is the representative of a 'forward' policy. Gladstone, abandoning Gordon at Khartoum, is the Little Englander. Is this again a question of degree?

This advertisement of 1887 illustrates the thesis that imperialist competition and the acquisition of colonies had a strong economic link.

Gladstone. Speech made during third Midlothian Campaign, 27 November 1879:

> I first give you, gentlemen, what I think the right principles of foreign policy. The first thing is to foster the strength of the Empire by just legislation and economy at home, thereby producing two of the great elements of national Power ... and to reserve the strength of the Empire, to reserve the expenditure of that strength for great and worthy occasions abroad.

Gladstone to the Mechanics' Institute, Chester, 12 November 1855:

> When then are colonies desirable? ... they are desirable both for the material and for the moral and social results which a wise

system of colonization is calculated to produce. At the first, the effect of colonization undoubtedly is to increase the trade and employment of the mother country. . . . But I do not concede that the material benefit of colonies is the only consideration which we are able to plead. Their moral and social advantage is a very great one . . . . It is the reproduction of the image and likeness of England – the reproduction of a country in which liberty is reconciled with order . . . it is because we feel convinced that our constitution is a blessing to us and will be a blessing to our posterity . . . that we are desirous of extending its influence.

Disraeli. Speech at the Crystal Palace, 24 June 1872:

They are proud of belonging to a great country and wish to maintain its greatness – that they are proud of belonging to an Imperial Country, and are resolved to maintain, if they can, their Empire – that they believe on the whole that the greatness and the Empire of England are to be attributed to the ancient Institutions of the land.

Disraeli. Speech at the Crystal Palace, 24 June 1872:

Well, what has been the result of this attempt during the reign of Liberalism for the disintegration of the Empire? It has entirely failed. But how has it failed? Through the sympathy of the colonies for the Mother Country. They have decided that the Empire shall not be destroyed, and in my opinion no Minister in this country will do his duty who neglects any opportunity of reconstructing as much as possible our Colonial Empire, and of responding to those distant sympathies which may become the source of incalculable strength and happiness to this land.

Gladstone to the House of Commons, 1855:

If Germany is to become a colonizing power, all I say is, 'God Speed Her'. She becomes our ally and partner in the great purposes of Providence for the advantages of mankind.

2 Lord Salisbury and the Theory of Splendid Isolation

It is frequently written that British foreign policy, in the late nineteenth century, was guided by two connected principles, 'Splendid Isolation', and the 'Balance of Power'. In the introduction of his book *Splendid Isolation* C. Howard comments, 'That Britain's conduct of her relations with other powers was formerly, and more especially during the nineteenth century ... governed by a principle policy or attitude ... of isolation – even splendid isolation, has been the view of many historians.' The idea that Britain, her vital links with the Empire secured by naval supremacy, could remain aloof from European affairs is linked with the existence on the Continent of a balance between the major powers. Significant expansion by any one state threatened Britain's safety, and she was particularly sensitive to political changes in areas bordering her essential sea routes. Hence the concern of British foreign ministers with the Mediterranean littoral in Southern Europe, and with countries bordering the Channel, in the North. Lord Salisbury, who as Foreign Secretary, and Prime Minister, dominated foreign affairs during the last quarter of the Century, is often considered the leading exponent of these policies.

To what extent was British policy consciously controlled by these principles, and to what extent was Lord Salisbury guided by them?

There is certainly widespread contemporary support for the opinion that, whether intentionally or not, Britain was isolated.

Lord Salisbury, 19 February 1886:
> In Europe we are isolated.
> *Hansard Parliamentary Debates*   3rd Series   Vol. CCXIV   1886   Col. 1775

Queen Victoria:
> Our Isolation is dangerous.
> LETTERS OF QUEEN VICTORIA
> *edited by Buckle   Murray, 1930*   *p.22*

The Kaiser, quoted in Swaine Memorandum, 20 December 1895:
> There is no question about it, the newspapers are right in saying –
> England is isolated. Now you have your hands full and everywhere
> you stand alone.
> *F/O. 64/1351*

Origins of the term
C. Howard comments:
> In the Nineteenth Century the normal meaning of the word
> 'isolation' when employed in an international context, was ... an
> embarrassing lack of friends among other powers on whom
> reliance could be placed for support in case of need.[1]

The 'Splendid' was added from the conviction that Britain's isolation
was a deliberate choice of policy, arising from her strength, and
Howard finds that the term was in common use from the last decades of
the century. *The Times* of 22 January 1896 had a cross heading
'Splendid Isolation' to report a speech of Chamberlain's in which the
British Minister quoted the Leader of the Canadian Commons, Foster:
'the great Mother Empire stood splendidly isolated.' Chamberlain
himself used the phrase in a speech made in Birmingham on 6 January
1902.

Chamberlain's speech, reported in *The Times*, 7 January 1902:
> I say, therefore, it is the duty of the British people to count upon
> themselves alone, as their ancestors did. I say alone, yes, in a
> Splendid Isolation, surrounded and supported by our kinsfolk.

Laurier (Leader of Canadian Opposition) in debate, 6 February 1896:
> For my part, I think splendidly isolated, because this isolation of
> England comes from her superiority.

Goschen (First Lord of the Admiralty) in a speech at Lewes, reported
in *The Times*, 27 January 1896:
> There may be the isolation of those who are weak and therefore are
> not counted because they contribute nothing, and there is, on the
> other hand, the isolation of those who do not wish to be entangled
> in any complication and will hold themselves free in every respect
> .... Our isolation is not an isolation of weakness, it is deliberately
> chosen ....

Was Britain really as aloof from Europe as these quotations imply?

> It might seem ... that Britain had little interest in Europe in this
> period, and in general this was true: seapower bred a sense of
> isolation from Continental problems. But the increasing over-
> extension of British commitments as against her resources ...

[1] SPLENDID ISOLATION *by C. Howard   Macmillan, 1967 p.1*

produced a considerable interest in European politics. If Britain were isolated in Europe her Empire became a standing invitation to attack and consequently ... there was a considerable incentive to assist in maintaining a balance of power .... Hence there was a basic British interest in opposing the hegemony of any one power. In Salisbury's eyes ... Germany was the only real potential menace to Britain .... As France and Russia were the weaker powers it was a British interest to avert any further deterioration in their position ....

But other interests led in an entirely opposite direction. The conflict with Russia over Constantinople, Central Asia and later over China, meant a certain identity of interest with the Central Powers, as did the increasing strain upon relations with France caused by Egypt. This, more than anything else, brought a direct involvement in European politics.

THE RELUCTANT IMPERIALISTS, vol. I
by C. Lowe   Routledge & Kegan Paul, 1967   *p.8*

It has been the traditional policy of England, according to most historians, to stand aloof from European affairs, so that in a crisis she might throw herself on the weaker side and prevent the hegemony of any one power or group of powers. This is the famous theory of the balance of power, a theory which I think should be discarded with reference to recent history, for the Story of European Diplomacy in the past fifty years or more completely contradicts it. Obviously England was, in the last half of the nineteenth century, interested less in the balance of power than in the maintenance of peace. In the heyday of her economic prosperity she had nothing to gain by war and had a good deal to lose even from war between other powers.

THE DIPLOMACY OF IMPERIALISM
by W. Langer   Knopf, New York, 1951   *p.789*

A more than superficial study of Salisbury's diplomacy disposed of the view that he was an isolationist in the sense of avoiding any formal contact with foreign nations. British interests in the last quarter of the nineteenth century came into conflict with those of other nations all over the world. Consequently no British foreign secretary could adopt a completely isolated position.

LORD SALISBURY AND FOREIGN POLICY
by J.A.S. Grenville   Athlone Press, 1964   *p.16*

Salisbury's own adherence to the principles of Splendid Isolation and balance of power has been questioned by historians:

Salisbury had spent longer at the foreign office than any other Foreign Secretary save Palmerston .... It is too often assumed that

'Splendid Isolation' was a supreme and satisfying aim. It would be more correct to regard it as in his mind an uncomfortable necessity imposed by the fluid state of continental politics. There can be little doubt that his preferences were in favour of the old friendship with France . . . and that to a lesser degree he would have viewed a rapprochement with Russia with much relief owing to our Indian and other Asiatic commitments. But his innate caution and realism convinced him that so long as the interpenetration of alliances subsisted . . . it would be a fatal blunder to commit Britain irrevocably to a place in one of the rival fronts.

But that he had no doctrinaire leaning towards isolation, and was fully alive to the danger of hostile coalitions is abundantly shown by his Mediterranean Agreements, his temporary alignment with the Triple Alliance, his overtures to Germany on the Turkish issue, his definite toleration of Chamberlain's experiments in foreign policy, his periodic efforts to agree with Russia. Above all, his relations with Bismarck in the last three years before the latter's fall dispose of the idea that he was unduly identified with the Balance of Power, for he then attached himself to what was already far the strongest combination instead of trying to redress the balance in Europe. There is only one motive which will explain the permutations of his policy in the eighties and nineties, namely his conviction that peace in Europe was Britain's greatest interest . . . the Machiavellian designs sometimes attributed to him, for instance holding aloof until the two main groups of Powers had been incited into conflict, and then profiting by their ruin – were quite accurately dismissed by his chief confidential secretary as 'grotesque'.

BRITAIN IN EUROPE, 1789–1914
by R. Seton-Watson   Cambridge, 1937   *p.594*

Salisbury . . . was much more European minded [than Gladstone]. Although he would never make a binding alliance if he could help it . . . he was always ready for bilateral collaboration in limited agreements. . . . Diplomacy to him was a market place in which you bought and sold and he was quite willing to offer to perform what he knew he could reasonably expect to carry out, in return for solid benefits. Hence the Mediterranean Agreements.

THE RELUCTANT IMPERIALISTS, vol. I
by C. Lowe   Routledge & Kegan Paul, 1967   *p.10*

Dislike of binding alliances did not prevent Salisbury from establishing . . . entente relationships. . . . Throughout this period, therefore, 'isolation' is too strong a term to apply to British policy.

FOUNDATIONS OF BRITISH FOREIGN POLICY
by H. Temperley and L. Penson   Cambridge, 1938   *p.516*

The tradition which ascribes to him an acquiescence, and even pride in isolation, is wholly negatived by his correspondence. The theories that have been built up upon that oft quoted phrase of 'splendid isolation' are a warning as to the dangers of unverified quotation. The words occur in a speech delivered by him at the Guildhall in November 1896. He was demurring to the moral denunciations which people in England were, at that time, heaping upon Russia and Austria. ... He reminded his audience that, placed geographically as those Powers were, their vital interests ... might be imperilled by a catastrophe in the South-East of Europe. It was not fair to expect in them 'the same emotional and philanthropic spirit with which you in your Splendid Isolation, are able to examine all the circumstances'. The phrase was used in a purely geographical sense.... And yet, divorced from their context and applied to a political idea with which they have no connection, the words have been used again and again as proof and embodiment in boastful form of a principle in his policy for which no other evidence exists. Isolation, in fact, is always referred to in those letters as an ultimate disaster, and his predecessors' record in having incurred it as an indisputable text for their condemnation.

But on the other hand, as has been seen, he refused to pursue his avoidance of it to what his continental friends looked upon as a logical conclusion. He was willing to rank England overtly in 'their group', to render to its members all services of national friendship; to engage, though somewhat reluctantly, for material co-operation with them in defence of certain already incurred obligations. But so far and no further ....

LIFE OF ROBERT, LORD SALISBURY, vol. IV
by G. Cecil   Hodder, 1921–32   *p.85*

The following quotations offer evidence from Lord Salisbury's own speeches and letters. They refer first to his general views, and then to particular key areas of foreign policy: the Eastern Question and the Mediterranean, and relations with Germany.

Salisbury to Sir W. White, 10 August 1887:
[I have] ... no belief whatsoever in that spirit of haughty and sullen isolation which has been dignified by the name of 'non intervention' .... We are part of the community of Europe, and we must do our duty as such.

Salisbury to Queen Victoria, 10 February 1888:
When war has once broken out we cannot be secure from the danger of being involved in it ... and if England was left out in isolation ... [of their] treating the English Empire as divisible booty by which their differences might be adjusted.

Memo to Lord Lansdowne, 29 May 1901:

Count Hatz Feldt speaks of our 'isolation' as constituting a serious danger for us. Have we ever felt that danger physically? If we had succumbed in the revolutionary war, our fall would not have been due to our isolation. We had many allies, but they would not have saved us if the French Emperor had been able to command the Channel . . . .

Salisbury. Speech at Caernarvon, 1888:

We think that a nation like ours should behave to other nations just as a man should behave to neighbours and equals among whom he may be dwelling . . . we are part of what has been well called the 'federation of mankind' . . . we are part of the Community of Europe and we must do our duty as such.

Salisbury to the House of Lords, 6 March 1871:

The whole of the old system of Europe may be said to have been swept away. We are looking into a future in which the equilibrium that governed Europe in past times has disappeared, and we have to reckon on new forces, new balances of power, possibly new enemies . . . . I trust on new and strengthened alliances . . . .

Hansard Parliamentary Debates   3rd Series   Vol. CCIV   1871   Col. 1360

Quarterly Review, October 1870:

Has it really come to this, that the disposal of the frontiers of France and Germany is a matter to us of the purest unconcern? Is not the crisis worth some little risk, even the risk of being thought by somebody to utter an unpalatable truth? We shall not conciliate the goodwill of our neighbours by refusing to contribute to the police of nations. . . . If their [Prussia's] intention is to reduce England to complete isolation . . . we doubt not they are preparing for themselves a severe condemnation from the English people. We only trust that they are not also preparing for England the national doom which always waits for the selfish and timid.

The Eastern Mediterranean, with the Balkans, was a key area in British foreign policy. Through it passed the sea routes that linked Britain with India and the Far Eastern Colonies. The political instability of the area, opening up the opportunity for an ambitious power to gain ascendency there, meant that the Foreign Office had continually to keep the situation under review, and general surveillance was interrupted by major crises, like that of 1875–78, when Britain was faced with the need for decisive action.

Memorandum from Lord Salisbury, 29 March 1878:

It cannot be otherwise than a matter of extreme solicitude to this

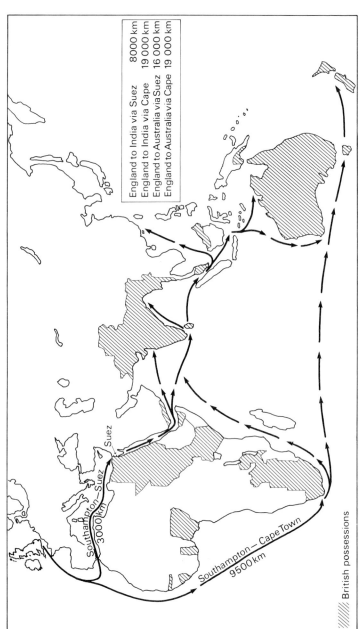

England to India via Suez	8000 km
England to India via Cape	19 000 km
England to Australia via Suez	16 000 km
England to Australia via Cape	19 000 km

Southampton – Suez
3000 km

Suez

Southampton – Cape Town
9500 km

///// British possessions

This map shows the importance of the Mediterranean as a sea route for Britain.

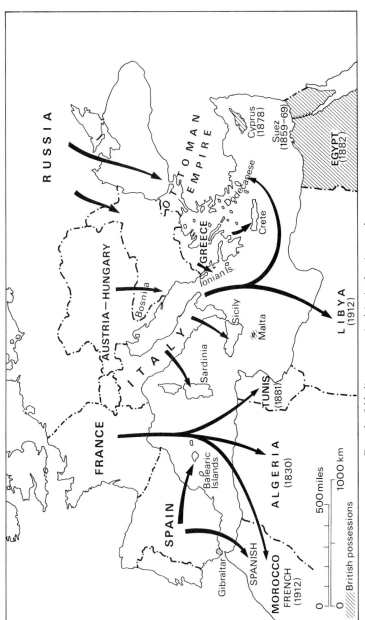

Growth of Mediterranean rivalries in the nineteenth century.

country that the Government to which this jurisdiction belongs [i.e. Control of the Straits] should be so closely pressed by the political outposts of a greatly superior power that its independent action and even existence is almost impossible.

Lord Salisbury, at Conservative Banquet, 27 July 1878:
Have we any right to throw away, to hide under a bush, to conceal in a corner, such power and influence as this, merely because we might at some distant time . . . add to our responsibility? I am told that, in the task of aiding and counselling the Ottoman Empire . . . we shall be hampered by the jealousy of other powers. I utterly refuse to believe it. When they find . . . that the one object we have in view is that peace and order shall be maintained . . . then I believe all idea of jealousy will vanish and that they will heartily co-operate with us in our civilizing mission.

Telegram to the Ambassador at the Porte, 25 January 1886:
Inform Porte that England has procured joint action of Powers to forbid attack by Greece on Turkey by sea.

The Mediterranean Agreements of February and December 1887 underline Salisbury's concern, since, despite vagueness and reservations, they were definite commitments to act with Italy and Austria. The first referred vaguely to co-operation against France in North Africa, and the maintenance of the status quo in the Mediterranean.

For the English and Italians the first Mediterranean Agreement was intended to check in advance any French design in Tripoli or Morocco. . . . At the same time it represented a connecting link between England and the Triple Alliance, which might, eventually, be extended. That Salisbury had this in mind is clear from the documents, and his apologist tells us of his great interest at that time in assuring the stability of the Triple Alliance and preventing Italy's withdrawal from it.
EUROPEAN ALLIANCES AND ALIGNMENTS 1871–1890
by W. Langer   Knopf, New York, 1950   p.401

The Second Mediterranean Agreement extended the maintaining of the status quo to the Near East. The freedom of the Straits and Turkish Authority in Asia Minor and Bulgaria were to be upheld, though this was not to be made known to the Turks.

Salisbury to the Ambassador at the Porte, 2 November 1887:
Germany, Austria and Italy have each communicated to us your eight bases [for extending the 1st Agreement] with an earnest recommendation that we should accept them. . . . My own

impression is that we must join, but I say it with regret .... But a thorough understanding with Austria and Italy is so important to us, that I do not like the idea of breaking it up on account of risks which may turn out to be imaginary.

Salisbury to the Austro-Hungarian and Italian Ambassadors, 12 December 1887:
> Most Secret
> Her Majesty's Government have considered the points commended to their acceptance by the identic notes of the Austro-Hungarian and Italian Governments.
>
> The three Powers have already communicated to each other their conviction that it is in their common interest to uphold the existing state of things upon the shore of the Mediterranean and the adjoining seas.

Salisbury to Mr Austin, commenting on an article in the *Standard:*
> I believe that England will fight in company with Austria, Turkey and Italy in case Russia should attack the Balkan States. ...

Salisbury to Queen Victoria, 10 February 1887:
> The English despatch – which, of course, is the only one binding on this country, is so drawn as to leave entirely unfettered the discretion of your Majesty's Government as to whether, in any particular case they will carry their support of Italy as far as 'material co-operation'. But short of a pledge on this subject, it undoubtedly carries very far the relations 'plus intimes' which have been urged upon us. It is as close an alliance as the Parliamentary character of our institution will permit. Your Majesty's advisers commend it on the whole, as necessary in order to avoid serious danger. If in the present grouping of nations ... England was left out in isolation, it might well happen that the adversaries who are arming against each other on the continent, might treat the English Empire as divisible booty, by which their differences might be adjusted, and, though England could defend herself, it would be at fearful risk and cost. ...

Another question of great importance was Britain's relationship with Germany, only recently united but rapidly developing not just the ambition, but the capability to become a world power. At times it seemed that she would be able to draw Britain into her Triple Alliance.

Salisbury to Lord Odo Russell, 10 April 1878:
> There are no countries who have so few rivalries and so many objects in common, and therefore there are none between whom understanding ought to be so good.

German Ambassador to Austro-Hungarian Ambassador 1888:
I am very much pleased with Lord Salisbury.

Its breach [i.e. a breach in the growing friendship of Britain and Germany] in Lord Salisbury's belief ... was mainly due to England's voluntary withdrawal from the diplomatic market place. A discriminating activity in exhibiting the value of her good will was the remedy to which he at once applied himself. He prepared the way by a private letter to Prince Bismarck – he recalled the friendliness of their earlier relations and expressed hopes of its renewal. He asked directly for the Chancellor's help in the removal of obstacles which Germany had raised to the immediate levying of an urgently required Egyptian loan.

LIFE OF ROBERT, LORD SALISBURY, vol. III
by G. Cecil   Hodder, 1921–32   *p.223*

Memorandum from Lord Salisbury on proposal for Britain to join Triple Alliance, 29 May 1901:
This is a proposal for including England within the bounds of the Triple Alliance. I understand its practical effect to be:
1. If England were attacked by two Powers – say France and Russia – Germany, Austria and Italy would come to her assistance.
2. Conversely, if either Austria, Germany or Italy were attacked by France and Russia, or if Italy were attacked by France and Spain, England must come to the rescue.

Even assuming that the Powers concerned were all despotic, and could promise anything they pleased with a full confidence they would be able to perform the promise, I think it is open to much question whether the bargain would be to our advantage. The liability of having to defend German and Austrian frontiers against Russia is heavier than having to defend the British Isles against France .... The fatal circumstance is that neither we nor the Germans are competent to make the suggested promises. The British Government cannot undertake to declare war for any purpose, unless it is a purpose of which the electors of this country would approve.

British Documents (B.D.) II 68–69

Finally it is worth noting the following comment:
It is a well known fact that Lord Salisbury and Lord Salisbury alone, is responsible for everything that is done and left undone in the region of foreign affairs. Neither the Cabinet nor the party exercises the slightest influence in that mare clausum.

THE FOREIGN OFFICE AND FOREIGN POLICY 1898–1914
by Z. Steiner   Cambridge, 1962   *p.24*

The Anglo-Japanese Treaty, 1902

3

The Anglo-Japanese Treaty of 1902 provides us with an excellent example of conflicting interpretation. How can Lord Strang, in his essay 'Britain in World Affairs' refer to it as a 'revolutionary turn in our foreign policy', while Lord Vansittart, in *The Mist Procession*, calls it a 'traditional stroke of British policy'? There is, of course, no doubt over the treaty's terms. As the extracts below will make clear, the problem comes in assessing its significance. On one side are contemporaries and historians who view it as a dramatic turning point when Britain abandoned isolation and commenced a series of alliances which were the steps leading to the First World War. On the other, as wide a group of observers see it as a small and not very dramatic extension of a well established policy.

Before we consider the interpretations it may be as well to put the treaty in its context. This is succinctly done by A.J.P. Taylor in *The Struggle for Mastery in Europe*: 'The issue that overshadowed all others was the Far East. China had taken the place of Turkey as the pre-eminent Sick Man, and between 1897 and 1905 the future of China determined the relations of the Great Powers.' This concept will be familiar, and has been referred to in the earlier chapters, but it is worth quoting Lord Salisbury's analysis of the problem, made in a speech given to the Primrose League in May 1898: '. . . the living nations will gradually encroach on the territory of the dying and seeds and causes of conflict among civilized nations will speedily appear'. In this case, the 'living nations', Germany, and particularly Russia, were encroaching on 'dying' China, threatening Britain's trading rights and her whole Open Door policy. Because of Russia's military pact with France, and Germany's Triple Alliance, it seemed that tensions in the Far East might bring war in just the way the Sarajevo murders did bring it in 1914.

Britain wished to defend her trading position, but this was becoming harder to do. As the First Lord of the Admiralty pointed out forcefully in a memorandum of 4 September 1901, Britain had fewer vessels in Chinese waters than the Fránco-Russian Alliance, and that very alliance made it too risky to reinforce the Far East fleet at the expense of

24

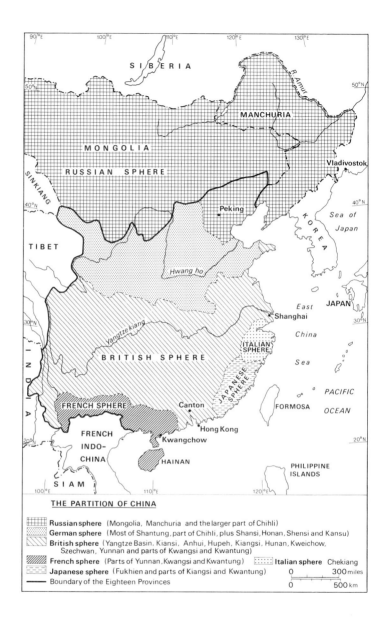

THE PARTITION OF CHINA

Russian sphere (Mongolia, Manchuria and the larger part of Chihli)
German sphere (Most of Shantung, part of Chihli, plus Shansi, Honan, Shensi and Kansu)
British sphere (Yangtze Basin, Kiansi, Anhui, Hupeh, Kiangsi, Hunan, Kweichow, Szechwan, Yunnan and parts of Kwangsi and Kwantung)
French sphere (Parts of Yunnan, Kwangsi and Kwantung) Italian sphere Chekiang
Japanese sphere (Fukhien and parts of Kiangsi and Kwantung)
Boundary of the Eighteen Provinces

0   300 miles
0   500 km

	France	Russia	Great Britain	Japan
Battleships	1 (2nd class)	5 (1st/2nd class)	4	6 (1st/2nd class)
Cruisers (1st class armoured)	2 (old)	6	3 (2 old)	7 (6 new)
Protected* (1st class)	2	–	4	–
Protected (2nd class)	5	1	8	10
Protected (3rd class)	–	–	1	14

The balance of naval power in the Far East.

the Mediterranean or Channel detachments. (The exact position is shown in the table above.) Britain, therefore, needed an ally, and found one in Japan, the strongest oriental naval power.

Does the treaty mark a real watershed in British foreign policy?

As has already been noted, the terms of the Alliance are not in dispute. It opened with the pacific statement: 'The governments of Great Britain and Japan, actuated solely by a desire to maintain the Status Quo, and general peace in the extreme East . . . hereby agree as follows.' It goes on to recognize China's independence, the powers promise co-operation, and, in the event of either becoming involved in war, neutrality. The critical article, over which so much controversy has arisen, is Article III: 'If in the above event [i.e. either ally becoming involved in war] any other Power or Powers should join in hostility against that ally, the other High Contracting Party will come to its assistance, and will conduct the war in common, and make peace in mutual agreement with it.'

In other words, the Alliance contains a clear and unequivocal military commitment, and in the documents quoted below, it will at once become clear that it is this fact that seemed so significant and so disturbing. Press reaction, for example, was unanimous in seeing the Treaty in this light.

The *Spectator*, 15 February 1902:
> The Spectator published an obituary edition for 'our fixed policy of not making Alliances'.

The *Daily News*, 13 February 1902:
> Not only does it destroy at a blow our 'Splendid Isolation'. It drags us into a Union where all the essential advantages seem to be on the other side.

* Protected cruisers had guns, but their hulls and decks were not armoured.

大日本帝國萬々歳

成歡襲擊
和軍大捷
之圖

1.

Three Japanese comments on their growing might:
1 & 2 illustrate the 1895 attack on Korea, and the defeat of China there.
3 (opposite) celebrates the victory over Russia at the Battle of Tshshima, 1905.

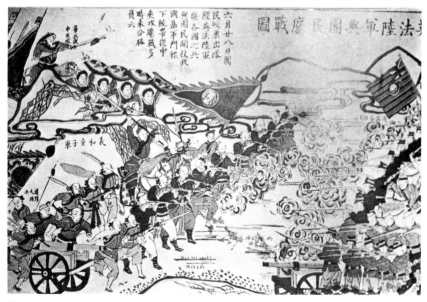

2.

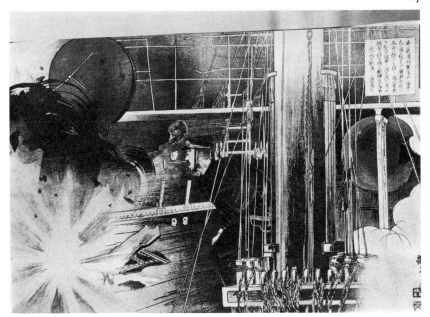

3.

The *Daily Chronicle*, 12 February 1902:
> Our Isolation, splendid or otherwise, is forsaken for a Dual Alliance.

The Times, 13 February 1902:
> ... a departure from the policy of isolation which England has so long pursued.

Many politicians reacted in the same way. In December 1901, before the treaty became public knowledge, A.J. Balfour wrote to Lord Lansdowne:
> Hitherto, we have always fought shy of any such engagements, and whether we have been right or wrong, we could at least say we were carrying out a traditional policy of isolation which had been proved successful in the past. We can say so no longer. The momentous step has been taken.

Defending the treaty in the House, on 13 February, Balfour was concerned not to deny the revolutionary nature of the policy but to justify it:
> So far as I am aware, every gentleman in this House is perfectly competent to understand the full weight of the grounds upon which we have made what I quite admit is ... a new departure.
> *Hansard Parliamentary Debates 4th Series Vol. CII 1902 Col. 1294*

His colleague in the upper house, Lord Lansdowne, recommending their Lordships to accept the Treaty, begged them to:

> Look at this matter strictly on its merits and not allow your judgment to be swayed by any musty formulas or old fashioned superstitions as to the desirability of pursuing a policy of isolation for this country.
>
> *Hansard Parliamentary Debates   4th Series   Vol CII   1902   Col. 1176*

The alarming departure from tradition was the gravamen also of the Opposition's attack. In the Commons, this was led by Mr Norman, M.P. for Wolverhampton South:

> The subject in question is an offensive and defensive Treaty of Alliance, involving a momentous change from the foreign policy of this country.
>
> *ibid. Col. 1273*

Lord Harcourt referred to:

> the departure from principles which have been consecrated by the traditions of nearly half a century.
>
> *ibid. Col. 1303*

Sir Edward Hamilton confided disapprovingly to his diary on 13 February:

> An agreement signed and sealed with Japan has transpired today, and taken everyone by surprise. It is a very new departure.

The same interpretation is argued by later historians, who continue to emphasize the military commitment as the key to the significance of the Alliance, and the basis for seeing it a revolution in British foreign policy.

> The departure from isolation was signalized by a Treaty of Alliance with Japan, which bound England in advance to potential action in the Far East. The Treaty was thus revolutionary.
>
> FOUNDATIONS OF BRITISH FOREIGN POLICY
> *by H. Temperley and L. Penson   Cambridge, 1938*   *p.521*

> The Anglo-Japanese Alliance marked Britain's first definite departure from what is called Splendid Isolation.
>
> *Hudson. Montagu-Burton lecture, Leeds 1955.*

The Treaty as a continuation of existing policy

We have already quoted Lord Strang's view of the affair, and it is typical of many others, but we ought now to look at the views of those observers alive at the time, and later commentators, who see the Treaty in a very different light. For example, if we return to the debates in Parliament, from which we have already quoted, we find some speakers

This postcard (c. 1902) illustrates the Russian view of British and American attitudes to the Russo-Japanese conflict.

putting forward a different interpretation. Lord Cranborne, speaking for the Government, defended the Alliance on the grounds that it was a small and logical extension of existing policy. He stressed the opening words of the Treaty, quoted earlier, emphasizing the anxiety of both Governments to maintain the status quo, and pointing out that several diplomatic arrangements had been made for that purpose, such as the 1900 Anglo-German Agreement, and the American Note. In answer to an objection raised by the Opposition, he rejoined:

What, then, Sir, is the situation? It is this: that in respect of the three main foundations of this Agreement – the Open Door, the Integrity of China, and the special position of Japan – we have before us, already agreed to, conventional arrangements by which almost every Power has endorsed these two principles in respect to China, and in which Russia herself has endorsed the principle which has regard to Korea. The House will follow the tendency of my argument. It is to show that this Agreement merely follows on principles which have already been accepted by almost every other Power .... Under these circumstances, the question which presented itself to the Government, and now presents itself to the House of Commons, is, could we not go one step further than we went in the previous convention and agreements which I have described to the House? Could we not go a little beyond the mere declaration of our policy of preserving the Open Door, and

C

*This French cartoon (c. 1904) illustrates the Asian view of 'The White Peril'
represented by Germany, Russia, Britain and France.*

maintaining the Integrity of China, by defining how that policy
must be carried out?
Hansard Parliamentary Debates 4th Series Vol. CII 1902 Col. 1283

The reasons for considering the Anglo-Japanese Alliance as a far less
significant event are not always as obvious as those for the contrary view
and the quotations therefore include the supporting arguments. For
example, Alan Taylor's pronouncement that the Alliance confirmed
splendid isolation needs explanation.

> ... The Alliance did not mark the end of British Isolation, rather it
> confirmed it. Isolation meant aloofness from the European
> Balance of Power, and this was now more possible than before.
> The British would no longer have to importune the Germans for
> help in the Far East; and therefore relations between them would
> be easier.
> THE STRUGGLE FOR MASTERY IN EUROPE, 1848–1918
> *by A.J.P. Taylor   Oxford, 1954*   *p.400*

One important contemporary, Kaiser Wilhelm II, who was very much
involved, agreed:

> The noodles seem to have had a lucid interval.
> THE DIPLOMACY OF IMPERIALISM
> *by W. Langer   Knopf, New York, 1951*   *p.780*

The next extract puts forward a different reason for viewing the Treaty in a diminished light:

To the historian it may well seem that insofar as Britain ever had a policy of isolation at all, that policy continued for several years after 1902. ... In 1906 Sir Edward Grey still upheld the view that 'Alliances, especially Continental Alliances, are not in accordance with our traditions.'

SPLENDID ISOLATION
by C. Howard   Macmillan, 1967   *p.96*

It will be noticed that both these historians imply the importance of being clear and accurate in use of terms. It is a point made by Langer and by Lowe. They also stress the need for accuracy in reading the terms of the Treaty and realizing the limit of its scope, and for understanding precisely what we mean by isolation. Lowe puts forward very clearly the arguments against seeing the Treaty in too significant a light, and he also suggests the explanation for such opposed interpretations of its importance.

It is misleading to confuse this alliance with the British position in Europe. The Anglo-Japanese Alliance made no appreciable difference here and it certainly did not end British 'Isolation' from the Continent. The Japanese agreement was a regional pact, to cope with the situation in China. ... It was not a general alliance. [He goes on to argue that by averting the need to weaken the fleet in European Waters it made a European Alliance unnecessary] ... in this sense [i.e. of avoiding such an Alliance] British Policy remained isolated until 1914. Despite the understandings with France and Russia there was no obligation to go to war, which makes nonsense of the thesis that there was a deliberate change in British Policy towards greater commitments in Europe and that this was initiated by the replacement of Salisbury by Lansdowne, and his Japanese Alliance in January 1902. ... Thus the general significance of 1902 has been overestimated as a turning away from a policy of isolation towards one of alliance. ... It was the exception not the rule.

THE RELUCTANT IMPERIALISTS, vol. I
by C. Lowe   Routledge & Kegan Paul, 1967   *p.249*

4 The 1904 Anglo-French Entente

In 1904 Britain signed the 'Entente Cordiale' with France. Mutual grievances, outstanding from centuries of rivalry in Europe and overseas, were resolved.

Both countries felt threatened by the turn of events in Europe and beyond. The Boer War, for example, had raised for Britain the spectre of a European Coalition against her. This had not materialized, but with growing threats to naval supremacy and the whole concept of the Pax Britannica, it made very clear the danger of standing aloof from the system of European Alliances. Initial moves towards Germany came to nothing, and the conviction grew that 'the Germans were playing a slippery game'. The alternative approach to France was eased by her own urgent need to reinforce her position.

The situation which gave rise to the 1904 Agreement is analysed by Bourne:

> The Germans still believed that England's quarrels with Russia were insoluble and would ultimately force her into an alliance on Germany's terms. So far, England had hardly shown sufficient respect for Germany; the German navy would help bring her to her senses. But this was a fatal mixture of blackmail and bluff – England could simply not afford to give in, while pride and miscalculation committed Germany to going on. The first major consequence of this new awareness of a supposed threat from the German naval programme was that it made the British Government . . . more responsive to approaches from France. For France, the Alliance with Russia had been of no help in the Fashoda crisis and with the signature of the Anglo-Japanese Alliance it threatened to embroil her in a war with England. One obvious step for France in these circumstances was to resist . . . the inclination of the Russian Government to make some positive retort to the Anglo-Japanese Alliance. Another was to try and avoid new clashes with England on her own account.
>
> THE FOREIGN POLICY OF VICTORIAN ENGLAND
> *by K. Bourne   Clarendon, 1970*   *p.181*

What factors contributed to the formation of the Entente?

Before considering how heavily the various factors – fear of Germany, the changed situation in the Far East, and lessening tension over colonies – weighed with the Government, it may be as well to deal with a rather different factor to which the Anglo-French rapprochement is sometimes attributed. How much influence had the Francophile Edward VII, 'the chief mischief maker' in his nephew's view? Warm tributes to his influence are readily found:–

> Son action, pour être humaine, et plus simple, n'en avait moins été réalle. Son bien veillance et son tact, il avait inspiré confiance.
>
> HISTORY OF FRANCE
> *by A. Maurois   Cape, 1949* *p.465*

> King Edward arrived in Paris on May 1st . . .. His reception, cool if not frigid at first, developed substantially into a very remarkable personal triumph, and the manifestations of public regard for him, both in respect to his individual and representative capacity, contributed largely to the improvement of the relations between the two countries.
>
> LORD LANSDOWNE – A BIOGRAPHY
> *by Lord Newton   Macmillan, 1929* *p.278*

Sir H. O'Beirne (Secretary at Paris Embassy) to Lord Lansdowne, 20 May 1903:

> I was greatly pleased with an observation made by a violent Anglophobe friend of mine. He said 'I can't think what has come over the population of Paris. The first day they behaved well, the second day they merely displayed interest, but the third day l'était attristant – ils ont acclamé le Roi'. This is testimony from a very hostile witness.

However:

> A legend arose in his life time, that British Foreign Policy was due to his initiative, instigation, and control. That was not so in my experience. He did not care for long and sustained discussion about large aspects of policy . . . .
>
> TWENTY-FIVE YEARS, vol. I
> *by Lord Grey   Hodder, 1925* *p.204*

Balfour to Lord Lansdowne, 11 January 1915:

> Have you looked through a small book on 'the Origins of the War' by Holland Rose? . . .
> I was . . . much surprised to see that he quite confidently attributes the policy of the Entente to Edward VII, thus embodying in serious historical work a foolish piece of gossip . . . .

Now, as far as I remember, during the years which you and I were his Ministers, he never made an important suggestion of any sort on larger questions of policy.

Turning to the factors analysed by Bourne, is there evidence that fear of Germany was driving France and Britain into friendship? (Naval policy is separately considered in Chapter 6.)

Two new factors were beginning to obtrude upon British consideration of policy. The first was that the French were becoming more amenable to agreement. The second was that the Germans were becoming very serious about their naval programme and World policy.

THE CRISIS OF IMPERIALISM
by R. Shannon   Hart-Davis MacGibbon, 1974   *p.339*

The month of December 1902 had seen the beginnings, however tentative, of the system of ententes. How far were they directed against Germany? For a growing party in the Foreign Office and probably for Chamberlain also, they were instruments of general diplomatic co-operation valuable as a check on Germany. But the policy of Balfour and Lansdowne was much more a response to the needs of the moment. It was knowledge of British weakness in Central Asia and Morocco that was bringing them to the realization that traditional policies must be given up, and some form of compromise with France and Russia sought. Fear of Germany was of only indirect importance. It added to the already heavy strain on the British position. . . . If relations with Germany had been better, Britain might not have felt so uneasy.

THE END OF ISOLATION
by G. Monger   Nelson, 1963   *p.114*

There is evidence of growing awareness of divergence of German and British interests:

The Two Powers (in 1901) were drifting apart, not as a result of a deliberate decision on the part of either, but because of the pressure of events, but these events reflected the underlying divergencies between their interests. The Germans had no real interest in China or Morocco, the British ... none in Austria or Italy. Britain was a great imperial and naval power. ... With France, on the other hand, relations steadily improved, once again not because of a deliberate decision, but because France was a great colonial power and it was found increasingly convenient to settle the colonial disputes at issue with her.

THE END OF ISOLATION
by G. Monger   Nelson, 1963   *p.43*

HER MOST GRACIOUS MAJESTY.

Our Queen and our Empress
Is greater and wiser
Than all foreign monarchs,
Including "der Kaiser."

These two illustrations depict the intense nationalism which was a factor in the deteriorating Anglo-German relations. The British cartoon depicts Queen Victoria; the German one the character of Alberich from Wagner's Nibelungen.

Lansdowne to Monson, 13 October 1901:
> Her interests are different from ours, and she has a habit of securing her pound of flesh whenever she confers or makes belief to confer a favour.
> *Lansdowne MSS Vol. IX*

Lansdowne to Lascelles, 28 August 1901:
> As for a 'complete understanding' between Germany and ourselves ... no-one could have striven harder than I to maintain such an understanding ... but (it) cannot be fruitful of good results unless the conduct of the parties to it proves to the world that they are in fruitful co-operation.
> *Lansdowne MSS Vol. XII*

Hamilton to Curzon, 16 January 1902:
> (Lansdowne is) coming round to the belief that they (the Germans) are a detestable race and the more we kick them the better friends we shall be.
> *Hamilton MSS Vol. IV*

Edward VII to Lascelles, 9 October 1902:
> It is inconceivable, the continual unfriendliness on the part of the German Government on every possible occasion.
> *Lascelles MSS Vol. IV*

Mallet to Bertie, 2 June 1904:
> A close understanding with France is a great safeguard for us ... our object ought to be to keep Germany isolated in view of her nefarious projects with regard to the Austrian Empire and Holland, to say nothing of this country.
> *Bertie MSS*

Memo by Lansdowne, 6 September 1903:
> A good understanding with France would not improbably be the precursor of a better understanding with Russia, and I need not insist upon the improvement which would result in our international position, which, in view of our present relation with Germany as well as with Russia, I cannot regard with satisfaction.
> *F/O 27/3765*

On the other hand:
Nicolson (Director of Military Intelligence) Memo 24, October 1902:
> It is to our advantage to interpose a German sphere of influence between the French sphere in Algeria and its extension westwards.
> *F/O 99/4000*

Balfour to Metternich, 9 June 1905:
> No sane person in England wishes to have a quarrel or war with
> Germany ... that would be an act of perfect lunacy.
> *G.P. XX No. 6855*

Sanderson to Lascelles, 5 March 1902:
> Whereas some time ago I had to explain often enough that there
> were certain things we could not expect of the Germans however
> friendly they might be, I have now, whenever they are mentioned
> to labour to show that the German government has in some
> material respects been friendly. There is a settled dislike to them,
> and an impression that they are ready and anxious to play us any
> shabby trick they can. It is an inconvenient state of things for there
> are a good many things in which it is important for both countries
> that we should work cordially together.
> *Lascelles MSS Vol. III*

German animosity was highlighted by reaction to events in South
Africa.

The Kaiser on the Jameson Raid:
> We must make great capital out of this story.
> *G.P. XI No. 2580*

Marschall (German Secretary of State) to Times Correspondent:
> It was necessary to give England a lesson [over the raid].

Delcassé, reporting a conversation between Wilhelm II and Noailles:
> The Boer War offered a unique opportunity which would not
> recur in a century for putting an end to the arrogance and
> aggression of England.

Deputy in Reichstag, 10 January 1902:
> The British army 'is a pack of thieves and brigands'.

> The disaster feared above all – a European Coalition – did not
> materialize, but the embarrassment and distraction of the war did
> lead to a weakening in Britain's military and diplomatic position.
> THE END OF ISOLATION
> *by G. Monger   Nelson, 1963*   *p.12*

Cambon to Henri Cambon, 16 April 1904:
> Without the war in the Transvaal, which bled Great Britain and
> made her wise, without the war in the Far East which made for
> reflection on both sides of the Channel and inspired in all a desire
> to limit the conflict, our agreements would not have been possible.
> *Correspondence II 134*

A caricature of Liberal leader, Sir Henry Campbell-Bannerman who decried Britain's 'methods of barbarism' during the war.

These contemporary cartoons illustrate the significance of the Boer War. Widespread European condemnation at home undermined British self-confidence and made the concept of alliance more appealing.

A grateful capitalist blacks the boots of bullying British soldiery – a German view of the war.

Events in the Far East drew Britain and France closer:

> The Impending Manchurian conflict threatened France – she must desert Russia or risk finding herself at war with Great Britain – the only way out was an Anglo-French reconciliation which might detach the British from Japan, or at least moderate both parties in the Far East. ... The Far East and the Far East alone caused the Anglo-French Entente.
>
> THE STRUGGLE FOR MASTERY IN EUROPE, 1848–1918
> *by A.J.P. Taylor Oxford, 1954* p.415

Lord Lansdowne:

> On 8th February 1904, the Japanese attacked the Russian fleet at Port Arthur. From that point, the French negotiations, after sticking in all sorts of ignoble ruts, suddenly began to travel at the rate of an express train.
>
> LORD CROMER
> *by the Marquis of Zetland Hodder, 1932* p.281

Lansdowne to Cromer, 26 December 1901:

> I have been struck by the comparative friendliness of the French ... their manners are better and in substance they are easier to deal with than the rest.
> *Lansdowne MSS Vol. XXXIX*

There is evidence of increasing awareness of the advantages of friendship with France.

Lansdowne to Monson, 13 March 1901, referring to Cambon's proposal:

> Our interests [in Morocco] he imagined were principally concerned with the coast, with which France did not desire to meddle. Would it not be possible ... for us to arrive at some amicable arrangement as to the extension of French influence in these unsettled districts?
> *F/O. Print Vol. 7817*

Edward VII to Eckardstein (German Diplomat) February 1902. Eckardstein 'Lebenserinnserungen':

> We are being urged more strongly than ever by France to come to an agreement in all colonial disputes.

Cromer to Lansdowne, 1 November 1903:

> We must manage to come to terms – we must not fail.
> *B.D. II*

Memo by Lansdowne, 10 September 1903:

> An all round settlement with France would ... be enormously to our advantage. It would be worthwhile to sacrifice something in

order to minimise the chances of future trouble with that country
.... A good understanding with France would not improbably be
the precursor of a better understanding with Russia, and I need
not insist upon the improvement which would result in our
international position, which, in view of our present relation with
Germany as well as Russia, I cannot regard with satisfaction.
F/O. 27/3765

Cromer to Lansdowne, 15 October 1903:
I cannot help regarding an understanding upon all pending
questions with France as possibly a stepping stone to a general
understanding with Russia and that this possibly again may
prepare the ground for some reduction in our enormous military
and naval expenditure.
LORD CROMER
by the Marquis of Zetland   Hodder, 1932   *p.274*

Eyre Crowe, 1 January 1907. Memo on the present state of British
relations with France and Germany:
A review of British relations with France ... reveals ancient and
real sources of conflict, springing from imperfectly patched up
differences of past centuries, the inelastic stipulations of anti-
quated treaties, or the troubles incidental to unsettled colonial
frontiers. ... When particular causes of friction become too acute,
special arrangements entered into succeeded as a rule in avoiding
an open rupture without, however, solving the difficulties, but
rather leaving the seed of further irritation behind. This was
eminently the case with France until and right up to the conclusion
of the Agreement of 8th April 1904.
P.R.O. Cab 37/8b No. 1

Comments on the agreement
Salisbury to Balfour, 9 November 1905:
In truth the French agreement was in its inception not a departure
from our previous foreign policy, but strictly in accordance with it.
For the last twenty years we have been engaged with different
powers, notably with Germany and with France, in adjusting
conflicting claims, and in bargaining so as to get rid of causes of
friction, and if I spoke about our agreement with France, I should
treat it rather as a development of past policy than as a new
departure.
Balfour MSS 48758

If I was silly enough to think the agreement no great shakes the
Germans were sharp enough to think otherwise .... The Kaiser
fired off one of his hostile speeches in under three weeks. Bismarck
had always tried to isolate France ... now she was doubly

emancipated by alliances east and west. Here too was an end of any continental alliance against Great Britain – our dread in past years. Naturally the Germans were incensed.

THE MIST PROCESSION

by Lord Vansittart   Hutchinson, 1958   *p.50*

The Times Leader, 9 April 1904:

The signature yesterday in London of the documents which embody a comprehensive agreement between this country and France, touching our mutual interests all over the globe, is an event of high historic importance. ... But we venture to say that the whole significance of the Agreement will be missed if it is jealously scrutinised as a mere barter of concessions from one country to the other. Its importance and its worth are really of a deeper kind. It is a landmark in the policy of the two nations, because it represents for the first time a serious attempt to see their worldwide relations steadily, and see them whole .... But transcending its significance in this respect is the value it must possess and the weight it must carry as a substantial pledge of the essential unity of our interests and desires. That value as a great factor in the peace of nations we believe it will retain, because it gives expression to the general and heartfelt wishes of the two great democracies whom it concerns.

The Times, 11 April 1904 from *Frankfurter Zeitung*, 10 April 1904:

France and England, before confirming their agreement must have satisfied themselves that what they were arranging with each other, was in no danger of encountering opposition or resistance on the part of Germany'.

The Times, 12 April 1904 from *Rheinish Westfalischer Zeitung*, 11 April 1904:

The result of the Entente is a complete change in the international situation, not to Germany's advantage. ... If Germany refrains from making claims she will go empty away from the partition of the world. ... The hour has come when Germany must secure Western Morocco from the Atlas to the sea.

The Times, 14 April 1904 from *Reichbote*, April 1904:

Germany is apparently not taken seriously in the councils of States. Where is Germany's place in the sun?

Reichstag debate, reported in *The Times*, 14 April 1904:

Most of the Deputies were very cautious in their references to the Anglo French Agreement ... the Radical, Herr Gothein thought that the Agreement indicated a certain coolness in the relations of England and Germany.

Lord Vansittart's assessment:

> The Agreement clinched in the spring of 1904 was no more than a bit of common sense. It settled our differences concerning Siam, West Africa, Madagascar, the New Hebrides – it ended a bicker about Newfoundland fisheries. ... More importantly the French gained a free hand in Morocco. ... For our part we gained French acquiescence in our special position in Egypt, so that we no longer needed the support of the Germans. Otherwise the Agreement tasted more like forbearance than cordiality. This truly was 'a turning point in History' .... Its results were immediately propitious. The British were no longer obliged to have long teeth in revue. We should have reciprocated by dropping 'Frog' from our vocabulary, but we were not quite supple enough for that.

THE MIST PROCESSION

by Lord Vansittart   Hutchinson, 1958   *p.50*

5 The Moroccan Crisis, 1906

Morocco provided the Kaiser with the opportunity to test the new Anglo-French Entente. The Sultan's position declined to a state which invited fresh foreign intervention. Germany was anxious to press her claims there, and Britain had agreed, in 1904, to allow France a free hand. When Wilhelm arrived in Tangiers he intended to challenge the new alliance. By demanding that France should dismiss Delcassé, the Minister who had signed it, and then agree to an International Conference on the future of Morocco, he hoped to demonstrate that when challenged, Britain would desert her ally.

Delcassé was dismissed, and the Conference met at Algeçiras – in an acrimonious spirit as *The Times* of 1 March 1906 makes clear: 'The French Correspondents are somewhat more hopeful today. Count Tattenbach abstained from making disagreeable remarks. After all that has taken place ... there is a disposition at Algeçiras to be thankful for small mercies, and when the second German delegate says nothing unpleasant for France, the barometer of the Conference tends to rise.' However, despite the Kaiser's confidence, Britain stood firmly by France, and Germany was obliged to allow considerable concessions to her rival.

What degree of commitment was assumed by the British Government when the Moroccan crisis broke?

> Renewed fear of German hostility put new life into the flagging entente, and this was especially true because the main German challenge was in Morocco. Britain had made the entente at the price of strategic concessions there which had ... left her vulnerable in the Western Mediterranean.
>
> THE END OF ISOLATION
> by G. Monger   Nelson, 1963   *p.188*

Cambon to Delcassé, May 1905:

> Si ... nous avions des raisons sérieuses de croire à une agression injustifiée de la part d'une certaine puissance le Gouvernement

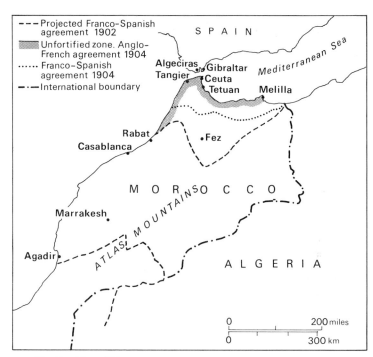

The Partition of Morocco.

britannique serait tout prêt à se concerter avec le Gouvernement
français sur les mesures à prendre.

Memo by Holstein, 4 April 1905:
  It is most unlikely that a conference will give Morocco to France
  against the vote of Germany.
  G.P. XX(11) No. 6601

Bülow to Kuhlmann, 6 April 1905:
  It is out of the question that the conference should result in a
  majority handing over Morocco to France.
  G.P. II No. 6604

Metternich to Bülow, 3 January 1906:
  The British people would not tolerate France's being involved in a
  war with Germany because of the Anglo-French Agreement.
  G.P. XXI No. 6923

Mallet to Bertie, 13 April 1905:
  When I saw Delcassé's resignation I wrote to Lord Lansdowne to
  say that I thought things looked serious for the entente and asked
  him what we should do supposing Germany pressed home her

D

victory and asked for a port. I urged him to let you tell the French Government that we would see them through. ... Lord Lansdowne answered 'consult Admiralty' so I went over to see Fisher. He said 'Of course the Germans will ask for Mogador and I shall tell Lord Lansdowne that if they do we must at least have Tangier'. He is a splendid chap and simply longs to have a go at Germany.
Bertie MSS Series A

Telegram from Lansdowne to Balfour, 23 April 1905:
Germany may press France for a port on the Moorish Coast. Admiralty think this fatal. May I advise French Government not to accede without giving us a full opportunity of conferring with them as to manner in which demand might be met?
Balfour MSS Add. MSS 49729

Salisbury to Balfour, 9 November 1905:
Circumstances no doubt have driven us in respect to France further than we intended. ... I think it very doubtful policy to drive Germany into the conviction that we are so absolutely estranged from her and so consolidated with France, that nothing is to be gained by seeking our goodwill.
Balfour MSS Add. MSS 49758

Grey to Bertie, 31 January 1906:
Diplomatic support we are pledged to give and are giving. A promise in advance, committing this Country to take part in a continental war is another matter and a very serious one. ... If France is let in for war with Germany arising out of our agreement with her about Morocco we cannot stand aside but must take part with France.
Bertie MSS

I did not think people in England would be prepared to fight in order to put France in possession of Morocco.
TWENTY-FIVE YEARS, VOL. I
by Lord Grey   Hodder, 1925   *p.80*

Minute by Hardinge on memo by Grey, 20 February 1906:
Yet in reality, he [Grey] was concerned about the European Balance in a way that no British Foreign Secretary had been since Palmerston. He endorsed the opinion of his leading adviser, 'If France is left in the lurch, an agreement or alliance between France, Germany and Russia in the near future is certain.
B.D. III No. 299

Grey to the House of Commons, 3 August 1914:
I must go back to the first Moroccan Crisis of 1906 . . . . I said then

This French cartoon (c. 1903) depicts the efforts of France,
Germany and Spain to dismember Morocco.

that I could promise nothing to any foreign power unless it was subsequently to receive the whole-hearted support of public opinion here. . . . I said, in my opinion if war was forced on France then upon the question of Morocco – a question which had just been the subject of agreement between this Country and France . . . that if out of that agreement war was forced upon France at that time, in my view public opinion in this country would have rallied to the material support of France. I made no promise, and I used no threats, but I expressed that opinion.

Hansard Parliamentary Debates 5th Series 1914 Vol. LXV   Col. 1810

Its sittings [Algeçiras Conference] began badly owing to the unacceptable terms put forward by the Kaiser and Holstein, who again had a case if they had known how to use it. Holstein assured his side that our support of France would 'remain platonic' . . . . For their part in the imbroglio the French unplatonically assumed that we did not love them whenever we pressed them to moderation.

THE MIST PROCESSION
by Lord Vansittart   Hutchinson, 1958   *p.57*

48

There is no doubt that the crisis strengthened the Entente, but how significantly? Did it, in effect, if not on paper, transform it into a firm military alliance?

Hitherto, the Entente, as negotiated by Lansdowne, had been a means of getting rid of French resentment. Lansdowne never thought of it as committing Britain necessarily to support of the French. Nor did he assume that the Entente with France conflicted with his constant efforts to get an equivalent entente with Germany.

THE CRISIS OF IMPERIALISM
by R. Shannon   Hart-Davis MacGibbon, 1974   *p.415*

The British regarded the Entente as the settlement of a tiresome irritation, not a fundamental shift in foreign policy. By ending Egypt and Morocco as topics of International conflict, it increased not ended their isolation.

THE STRUGGLE FOR MASTERY IN EUROPE, 1848–1918
by A.J.P. Taylor   Oxford, 1954   *p.413*

The Fall of Delcassé had shaken British faith in France, Lansdowne declared 'it was disgusting'. But he blamed French feebleness rather than German bullying, and he drew the moral that France was useless as a partner, not that Germany should be resisted. The ending of the Russo-Japanese war also made the Entente less necessary, and there was very little contact between Great Britain and France in the autumn of 1905.

THE STRUGGLE FOR MASTERY IN EUROPE, 1848–1918
by A.J.P. Taylor   Oxford, 1954   *p.435*

Neither the French nor the British entered into the question with any deliberate idea of emerging as an anti-German bloc.

THE CRISIS OF IMPERIALISM
by R. Shannon   Hart-Davis MacGibbon, 1974   *p.342*

Even the Germans themselves viewed the situation calmly.

Metternich (German Ambassador in London), 2 June 1903. Despatch to Berlin:

The English Government has the satisfying feeling of having one opponent fewer. But reconciliation with one opponent does not necessarily mean enmity with a third. On the contrary I know it does not wish to destroy, but maintain the wire to Berlin.

Bülow (German Chancellor). Speech to Reichstag:

An attempt to remove a number of difficulties by peaceful methods. We have nothing from the standpoint of German interests to object to in that.

What evidence is there, that by supporting France at Algeçiras, Grey was 'working towards a new doctrine of the European balance of Power', which was in fact 'a fundamental change'?

> Grey had assumed that an Anglo-German rapprochement could safely follow a successful conclusion of the Algeçiras Conference. The fact that ... this proved not to be so led him to examine more closely the assumptions lying behind his policy. ... Germany was now definitely identified as the threat to the European balance. 'The Germans' he minuted on 9th June, 'do not realize that England has always drifted or deliberately gone into opposition to any power which establishes a hegemony in Europe.' All the elements of his policy – his support for the Entente, his search for a Russian Agreement, his determination to uphold the balance of power – now fall into place ... he used the most far reaching language to the French in order to allay their fears of an Anglo-German rapprochement. When on 20th June Cambon stated that the King's meeting with the Kaiser on the Continent would cause apprehension in France, Grey assured him that 'if anything arose which made it necessary to choose between France and Germany, public opinion here would be as decided on the French side as ever.' ... These assurances by Grey were his first official recognition of the changed conception of the Entente. ... They were promises extending in scope to the entire policies of England and France. ... Now its purpose was to protect France against Germany in order to maintain the European balance of power, the preservation of French strength became in itself essential to British Security.
>
> THE END OF ISOLATION
> *by G. Monger   Nelson, 1963*   *p.300*

Eyre Crowe. 'Memo on the present state of British relations with France and Germany', 1 January 1907:

> When the signature of the Algeçiras Act brought to a close the first chapter of the conflict respecting Morocco, the Anglo-French Entente had acquired a different significance from that which it had at the moment of its inception. Then there had been but a friendly settlement of particular outstanding differences, giving hope for future harmonious relations between two neighbouring countries that had got into the habit of looking at one another askance; now there had emerged an element of common resistance to outside dictation and aggression, a unity of special interests tending to develop into active co-operation against a third Power. It is essential to bear in mind that this new feature of the Entente was the direct effect produced by Germany's effort to break it up,

and that failing the active or threatening hostility of Germany, such anti-German bias as the Entente must be admitted to have at one time assumed, would certainly not exist at present, nor probably survive in the future . . . .

That the result was a very serious disappointment to Germany has been made abundantly manifest by the turmoil which the signature of the Algeçiras Act has created in the Country. The time which has since elapsed has, no doubt, been short. But during that time it may be observed that our relations with Germany, if not exactly cordial, have at least been free of all symptoms of direct friction, and there is an impression that Germany will think twice before she now gives rise to any fresh disagreement.

BRITISH DOCUMENTS ON THE ORIGIN OF THE WAR, vol. III
by Gooch and Temperley   London 1926–36   *p.397*

Comments of historians

Britain still preserved a relative freedom of action and would fain have played mediator in the interests of peace. Indeed ... she showed an increasing readiness to apply in her relations with Germany the same methods of investigation and discussion which had produced successive détentes with Japan, France and Russia.

BRITAIN IN EUROPE, 1789–1914
by R. Seton-Watson   Cambridge, 1937   *p.611*

The question that Grey had to face was: Would, or should, Britain go to war with Germany for the sake of the balance of power in Europe, which in practice meant the preservation of France as a great Power, and as a necessary corollary, the preservation of the Franco-Russian Alliance? And if the answer to this question was 'Yes', could Britain make the necessary contribution in the application of Power? These were the questions at the heart of British foreign and naval and military policy in the years from 1906. The answers arrived at were, first, that Britain would go to war to preserve France. ... Secondly it was decided that for this purpose a sufficient military force would be despatched to the left wing of the French Order of Battle. ... These conclusions were virtually fore-ordained by the end of the Algeçiras Conference in March 1906.

THE CRISIS OF IMPERIALISM
by R. Shannon   Hart-Davis MacGibbon, 1974   *p.414*

Contemporary comment

General memo (Berlin) reviewing 1906 situation:

The Conference at Algeçiras has removed the last doubt with regard to the existence of an Entente between France, Great

Britain and Russia. ... To meet the British plan of sending an expeditionary Force of 100,000 men to the Continent, it would be necessary to make a better formation of reserves. ...

Obtained from 'a reliable source' by M. Etienne (Min. of War):
Neither ridiculous shriekings for revenge by French chauvinists, nor the Englishmen's gnashing of teeth nor the wild gestures of the Slavs will turn us from our aim of protecting and defending Deutschum [German Influence] all the World over.
DIPLOMATIC DOCUMENTS ON THE ORIGINS OF THE WAR
H.M.S.O., 1915   *p.131*

Metternich to Bülow, 23 August 1906:
English policy is founded on co-operation with France ... only if English policy succeeds in making a Franco-German agreement will English friendship be politically useful to us.
G.P. XXXII No. 7198

Press Reaction. *The Times* Leader, 2 April 1906:
Germany has failed however, to attain what was probably her chief aim ... she has not succeeded in undermining the Anglo-French Entente. ... On the contrary she has unintentionally strengthened our entente cordiale with France during the Conference by giving us an opportunity of proving by Acts that we place debts of honour above considerations of material interest.

The Times Leader, 13 April 1906:
Everything goes to show that our joint action with France at Algeçiras has materially strengthened the Anglo-French Entente, and we have more than once expressed the hope ... that the Entente may be supplemented by an Anglo-Russian understanding. If this should prove to have been even indirectly promoted by the Algeçiras Conference, that gathering will have made very considerably for the peace of the World .... In this Country we have from the first regarded the Algeçiras Conference as a test of Germany's professions of friendship. The concessions which she made were from this point of view most welcome, though their grace and effectiveness would have been immeasurably advanced had they been made earlier. We trust that her more friendly attitude at the close of the Conference may pave the way to an improvement of her relations both with France and with this Country.

It was a true crisis, a turning point in European history. The British contemplated military intervention on the Continent for the first time since 1864.
THE STRUGGLE FOR MASTERY IN EUROPE, 1848–1918
by A.J.P. Taylor   Oxford, 1954   *p.441*

6 Anglo-German Naval Rivalry

With the new century, Britain and Germany began to drift apart, despite efforts on both sides to prevent estrangement. Naval rivalry is often cited as a major factor in the hostility between them.

Britain's economic strength, and her position as a world power depended on her Empire. The safety of her Empire, and of her links with it, depended not just on possession of a navy, but upon naval supremacy. She had to be sure that colonies and trade routes in any part of the world could be defended against not only any nation, but any combination of nations. The attention paid by British statesmen to the Mediterranean, for example, illustrates the concern with one sea link in the vital chain of communications.

For most of the nineteenth century, Britain's supremacy at sea was unquestioned. The situation began to change as the Continental Powers started to look outward from Europe. As they gained colonies, they needed navies, and in naval building Germany began to acquire a strength that alarmed Britain. Technical improvements, making older ships obsolete, increased costs alarmingly, overwhelming superiority became impossible to maintain and the 'Two Power Standard' by which the British fleet was to outnumber the combined fleets of the second and third naval powers, was increasingly hard to achieve.

What part did naval rivalry play in the deteriorating relations between Britain and Germany?

In attempting to weigh the part played by naval rivalry in destroying good relations between Germany and Britain, and bringing them to the point of war, subsidiary questions can be posed. Did the initial hostility arise from the construction of the German fleet, and was that fleet vital to German interests? What evidence is there of an arms race, centred around the Dreadnought? Did naval rivalry create a climate in which war became, increasingly, the anticipated end?

That naval supremacy was felt to be vital to Britain is not seriously in doubt.

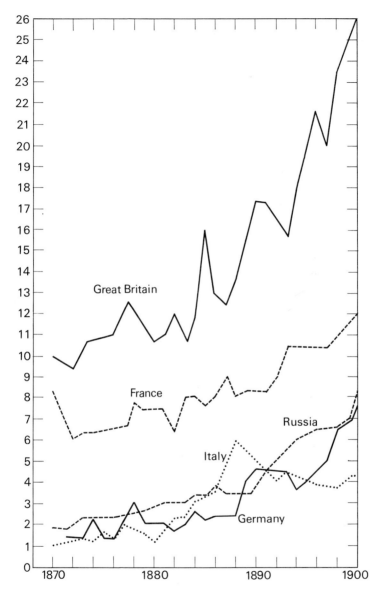

The rising expenditures of European Powers on their naval establishments (in £m).

	1870	1880	1890	1900	1910	1914
Germany	1·2	2·4	4·6	7·4	20·6	22·4
Austria–Hungary	0·8	0·8	1·2	1·8	2·8	7·6
France	7·0	8·6	8·8	14·6	14·8	18·0
Great Britain	9·8	10·2	13·8	29·2	40·4	47·4
Italy	1·4	1·8	4·6	4·8	8·2	9·8
Russia	2·4	3·8	4·4	8·4	9·4	23·6

Naval estimates of the Great Powers, 1870–1914 (in £m).

The nineteenth century had been the age of the 'Pax Britannica'. During the long Victorian peace, Britain, secure in her economic strength and her rule of the seas, had built herself the largest empire in the world. ... Even at its greatest, British power had depended upon the unwillingness and inability of the European nations, preoccupied in the affairs of the Continent, to challenge her effectively overseas. When, towards the end of the Century, this condition ceased to hold, Britain ceased to enjoy unchallenged superiority. ... Britain was everywhere faced with new rivalries, new pressures. ... The British navy had lost undisputed command of the Mediterranean; from this fact all else flowed'.

THE END OF ISOLATION
by G. Monger   Nelson, 1963   *p.1*

Eyre Crowe. Memorandum on the present state of the British relations with France and Germany, 1 January 1907:

The general character of England's foreign policy is determined by the immutable conditions of her geographical situation on the ocean flank of Europe as an island State with vast overseas colonies and dependencies whose existence and survival as an independent community are inseparably bound up with the possession of preponderant sea power.

P.R.O. Cab 37/86 no. 1

Hardinge (Permanent Under Secretary at Foreign Office) to Bryce (Ambassador in Washington), 4 June 1909:

As long as we maintain our undoubted supremacy at sea, we need have no cause for alarm even if we find ourselves once more in a position of complete isolation, but supremacy at sea is a condition which must be regarded as an absolute sine qua non.

Hardinge MSS Vol. 17

James Thursfield in the *Quarterly Review* of October 1893:

> To all other powers a strong navy is more or less a luxury, useful
> for certain subordinate purposes. .... To England alone it is from
> the very nature of the case an absolute and primordial necessity.

> We're a maritime nation – we've grown by the sea and live by it, if
> we lose command of it, we starve. We're unique in that way, just as
> our huge Empire, only linked by the sea, is unique. ...
>
> *Spoken by Davies, in* THE RIDDLE OF THE SANDS
> *by Erskine Childers*

How far did Germany begin to feel that a powerful navy was vital to her present interests, and her future development?

G. Steevens (English Correspondent) reporting a young German, 11
October 1897:

> Our Kaiser is one of the greatest men in history .... He sees the
> time for a Continental policy is gone by; first of the Germans he
> pursues a world policy. ... The strong navy is the essential
> condition of world policy.
>
> THE GREAT NAVAL RACE
> *by P. Padfield   Hart-Davis MacGibbon, 1974*   *p.33*

Memo by Von Tirpitz, 13 February 1896:

> If we intend to go out into the world and strengthen ourselves
> commercially, by means of the sea, then if we do not provide
> ourselves simultaneously with a certain measure of sea power, we
> shall be creating a perfectly hollow structure.
>
> MY MEMOIRS, vol. I
> *by Von Tirpitz   Hurst and Blackett, 1919*   *p.63*

Von Tirpitz to Von Stosch, 21 December 1895:

> In my view Germany will swiftly sink from her position as a great
> power in the coming century if these maritime interests are not
> brought to the forefront energetically, systematically and without
> any loss of time.
>
> MY MEMOIRS, vol. I
> *by Von Tirpitz   Hurst and Blackett, 1919*   *p.60*

Von Tirpitz to Wilhelm II, 1898:

> The essential connection which exists, especially between sea
> power and the development of commercial interests, will in future
> be even more sharply delineated. In the economic struggle which
> the nations must wage in the coming century it will become even
> more necessary to defend the maritime interests of Germany by
> armed force.

This postcard was issued on the occasion of the Kaiser's launching of the SS Imperator.

The German Fleet bore no reasonable relation to Germany's growing trade and overseas interests. Germany was the second power in the world so far as foreign trade was concerned. Yet in sea power she ranked not only behind England, France and Russia, but behind Italy.

What evidence is there that, from the first, Germany realized and even deliberately planned the challenge her policy offered to Great Britain?

Kaiser in a speech at Hamburg, 1897:
  The Trident belongs in our fist.

Empress Frederick to Queen Victoria:
  William's one idea is to have a navy which is larger and stronger than the British navy.
  LETTERS OF THE EMPRESS FREDERICK
  edited by Sir F. Ponsonby   Macmillan, 1928   *p.447*

Kreizzeitung, 9 October 1897:
  Germany must aspire to a naval power which will make her an important ally for the other great naval states if England should assume an attitude of selfish predominence in reckless disregard of all interest except her own.

Von Tirpitz to Kaiser, June 1897:
> Very Secret
> 2 For Germany the most dangerous enemy at the present time is England. She is also the enemy against whom we must have a certain measure of Fleet Power as a political power factor . . . .
> 4 Our fleet is to be so constructed that it can unfold its highest battle functions between Heligoland and the Thames.

August Bebel, German Socialist Leader, reported in *The Times*, 14 January 1908:
> The German government will never be able to eradicate from the minds of the English people the idea that the German navy is directed against England, if only because there is no other adversary against which it could be used.

Von Tirpitz, in reply to Bebel, reported in *The Times*, 16 January 1908:
> We are building our fleet against no one.

Wilhelm II to Lord Tweedsmouth, 14 February 1908:
> It is absolutely nonsensical and untrue that the German Naval Bill is to provide a navy meant as a 'Challenge to British naval supremacy'. The German fleet is being built against nobody at all. It is solely built for Germany's needs in relation to that country's rapidly growing trade.

Von Tirpitz to German Naval Attaché in London, 16 November 1899:
> We must know if the English government plans to introduce to Parliament any naval proposals as a result of the German 'Novelle' and if the English government considers us an opponent at sea, or whether it has made reference to the German fleet.

Bülow – draft of speech, 27 March 1900:
> In 1897, as the fleet measure was introduced, the possibility of a clash with England did not appear seriously to be at hand. But I dare not conceal that since then circumstances have so changed that today such an eventuality is within the bounds of possibility.

Passage accompanying the new naval Law, 1900:
> To protect Germany's sea trade and colonies in the existing circumstances, there is only one means. Germany must have a battle fleet so strong that even for the adversary with the greatest sea power a war against it would involve such dangers as to imperil her position in the world.

It was natural enough that Germany should want a respectable navy, but not one of such a type and size as she insisted on building. The basis of her construction programme was Von Tirpitz's theory that the German navy must be so strong that not

even the greatest naval power could risk attacking Germany. The short range envisaged for the battle fleet confirmed that it was designed to operate in the North Sea and against Great Britain.
THE FOREIGN POLICY OF VICTORIAN ENGLAND
by K. Bourne   Clarendon, 1970   *p.181*

British reaction to German naval expansion was strong. Was it strong enough to account for the acceleration in her own shipbuilding programme, and particularly her search for a new class of battleship?

Erskine Childers wrote *The Riddle of the Sands* to try to awaken an awareness of the threat Germany presented. His character Carruthers speaks of Germany:

Impregnably based on vast territorial resources which we cannot molest ... our great trade rival of the present, our great naval rival of the future, she grows and strengthens and waits, an evermore formidable factor in the future of our delicate network of Empire ... radiating from an island whose commerce is its life and which depends even for its daily ration of bread on the free passage of the seas.

Confidential memo by the Admiralty, August 1902:

An examination of the German ship yards and shipbuilding establishments gives rise to some very serious reflections .... That the naval power of Germany is already formidable no one who has the slightest acquaintance with the German fleet will deny. That it is destined in the near future to become more powerful than it is at present is clear. ... Against England alone is such a weapon as the modern German navy necessary, against England, unless all available evidence and all probability combine to mislead, that weapon is being prepared.

'Vanity Fair' in the *Sun*, 17 November 1904:

Day and night Germany is preparing for war with England. ... If the German fleet were destroyed the peace of Europe would last for two generations.

Fisher to Arnold White, 6 August 1902:

The German Emperor may be devoted to us, he can no more stem the tide of German commercial hostility to this country of ours than Canute could keep the North Sea from wetting his patent leather boots! It's inherent. Their interests everywhere clash with ours.

German Ambassador to Wilhelm II, January 1903:

As long as I have known England, I have never observed here such bitterness towards another nation as at present exists towards us.
G.P. XVII

The Times, 22 November 1907, quoting the Paris *Aurore*:
> The exposé of the new naval programme of the Empire shows that the strength of the German navy will be doubled between 1907 and 1914. There can be no doubt that this formidable fleet ... is directed mainly against England.

The *People*, 12 January 1908:
> A German fleet is a luxury not a national necessity, and is not therefore a fleet with a pacific object.

Prince Henry of Prussia to Fisher, 28 March 1908:
> Never mind the Times, never mind the Press. Let them be d—d. He who tries to prove that Germany is or will be a menace to England, or that Germany intends to be aggressive is certainly quite in the wrong and (pardon me) a lunatic.

Not all Englishmen took things too seriously though:
> The news from home was more entertaining. The Kaiser had come to Britain in the autumn of 1907 and made, anent the German naval programme, soothing sounds. . . . To show that there was no ill feeling Lord Tweedsmouth, First Lord of the Admiralty – and Neptune only knows how he got there for he was perfectly potty – had communicated our naval estimates to the Kaiser before submitting them to Parliament.
> THE MIST PROCESSION
> *by Lord Vansittart   Hutchinson, 1958*   *p.77*

Finally, what evidence exists of the naval race, and what evidence is there that naval rivalry played a significant part in bringing about war?

Sir Wm White, K.G.B. in *The Times*, 27 December 1906:
> Remarkable advances have been made in German shipbuilding during the last ten years . . . .
> British supremacy at sea requires the construction and maintenance of numerous and more powerful fleets. It has been and must remain a cardinal feature in naval policy, that our warship building capacity should be ... superior to that of other maritime nations.

Lascelles to Lansdowne, 25 April 1902:
> The German navy is professedly aimed at that of the greatest naval power – US.
> *Lansdowne MSS Vol. III*

Chamberlain Memorandum, 14 January 1906:
> Whatever Count Bülow may say, her navy is a standing menace to this Country. It has been openly commended to German patriotism in the German press for this reason.
> *Chamberlain MSS Box 17*

NEW BOOKS.

SOME LIVELY RECOLLECTIONS.

MEMORIES OF SIR LYON 1844–1890. By Sir Algernon West. (Nelson. 2s. net.)

GERMANY ON THE WATER.

The photographs are of the German fleet, which during the early days of the war furnished, in readiness for war at East and West submarines. The top row shows the first-class battleships steaming out to sea and torpedo boats. — the lower one the German submarines and torpedo boats.

MISCELLANY.

SHACKLETON'S SHIP.

THE ENDURANCE LEAVES THE THAMES.

The photograph gives a good general view of one of the latest of the English battleships, the Endurance, which is attached to the expedition of Sir Ernest Shackleton, is now leaving the Thames.

Riverside Greetings.

THE SALFORD COUNCIL.

£25,000 FOR TRAMS.

While the famous slogan 'we want eight and we won't wait' reflects British determination to maintain naval superiority, nevertheless the naval race, financed by the taxpayer, was unpopular.

Metternich, in a despatch to Berlin:
The real cause of tension is the growing importance of our navy.

Balfour, in an article in *Nord und Sud*, July 1912:
Without a superior fleet, Britain would no longer count as a power.
Without any fleet at all Germany would remain the greatest power
in Europe.

Memo from Lord Grey to Edward VII, July 1908:
If the German navy ever became superior to ours, the German
army can conquer this Country. There is no corresponding risk of
this kind to Germany for however superior our fleet was, no naval
victory would bring us nearer Berlin.
B.D. VI No. 779

Angst to Tyrell, 20 December 1911:
We are told in secret by the government our [Germany's] only
chance against the more powerful English fleet would be to be 'two
months in advance with our preparation at the moment of
striking'. The Minister added that they were straining every nerve
to be thus prepared.
P.R.O. F.O. 800 104

Colonel Trench, in a despatch to the Admiralty, 1908:
I dare not finish without recording that I believe at the bottom of
every German heart today is rising a faint and wildly exhilarating
hope that he might even wrest command of the sea from England.

Upon the wall behind my chair I had an open case fitted, within
whose folding doors spread a large chart of the North Sea. On this
chart every day a Staff Officer marked with flags the position of the
German Fleet. Never once was this ceremony omitted until the
war broke out . . .. I made a rule to look at my chart once every day
when I first entered my room. I did this less to keep myself
informed . . . than in order to inculcate in myself and those working
with me a sense of ever present danger.
WORLD CRISIS, vol. IV
by W. Churchill   Butterworth, 1923   *p.72*

Memo. Board of Admiralty, 1 February 1906:
Battleships remain the surest pledge this Country can give for the
continued peace of the world.
P.R.O. Adm. 116/866B

Lord Tweedsmouth to Campbell-Bannerman, 21 November 1906:
Our firm reliance must be placed in a continuity of foreign and
naval policy. All governments for the last twenty one years have

accepted and acted up to the Two Power Standard, and it is not to be lightly abandoned now.

C.B. MSS   *p.311*

The Times, 27 December 1906, quoting a speech by A. Lee in the House of Commons:

According to the facts published by the Admiralty, the Dreadnought had more than twice the gunpower of any existing battleship and sufficient speed and coal endurance to out-manoeuvre any battleship afloat. The first country that completed a fleet of Dreadnoughts would ipso facto secure command of the sea. ... We were bound if we intended to retain our naval supremacy to retain a supremacy in ships of the new type.

Balfour to the House of Commons, quoted in *The Times*, 27 December 1906:

A squadron of four of these battleships are almost invulnerable by any existing naval combination. Therefore, if we are really to keep pace with other nations as regards battleships, we shall have to build this new type at a rate equal to any two powers.

Fisher, 10 February 1909:

The only issue is the number of Dreadnoughts! Why? Because ... no matter how many of the Canopus class, for instance, try to fight a Dreadnought, the Dreadnought, at a range beyond the Canopus gobbles them all up! Its the armadillo and the ants – the armadillo puts out its tongue and licks up the ants. Therefore can we sleep quiet in our beds in view of the certainty that the Germans can have twenty-one against our eighteen in April 1912, when they mean to fight?

Sea Lord's memo, January 1909:

We wish to emphasize the point that Great Britain's eighteen to Germany's seventeen Dreadnoughts in 1912 is not considered in any way adequate to maintain command of the sea in a war with Germany. ... We therefore consider it of the utmost importance that power should be taken to lay down two more armoured ships in 1910–1911, making eight in all.

Wilson to Esher, 1 August 1911:

We are in the satisfactory position of having twice as many Dreadnoughts in commission as Germany and a number greater by one unit than the whole of the rest of the World put together! I don't think there is the very faintest fear of war! How wonderfully Providence guides England ....

Time and the Ocean and some Guiding Star
In High Cabal have made us what we are.

RUBBING IT IN,
OR, THE CONTINGENT SENTENCE.

JUDGE: "I sentence you to the second place for life—and if you answer back I'LL GIVE YOU TEN YEARS MORE!"

Mr. Churchill's Navy Estimates not only provide for the laying down of four keels to Germany's two, but threatens a still further increase of the ratio " if the existing programmes of the other Powers are increased."

DAILY DISPATCH, FRIDAY, MAY 17, 1912.

THE ELASTIC ESTIMATES,
OR, BEATEN IN THE STRETCH.

FRITZ: "Himmel! De more I squeeze to stretch mein own boat, de bigger it makes de odder one!"

Mr. Churchill states that in answer to the increased German naval expenditure he will bring in his promised "supplementary estimates for ships and men."

Germany; determination to increase her navy and Britain's determination to retain naval supremacy, created great financial burdens for both powers.

At the end of 1911, word reached Wilhelm that the British government was prepared to help Germany acquire further colonies in return for concessions in the naval question. Could such a proposal, backed up by embassies like Haldane's, have saved the situation?

Tyrell to Grey:
> The race in naval armaments is the disturbing factor. To get rid of this should be the main object in view. Political relations will improve automatically after that.

Cassel to Ballin[1], 3 February 1912
> If on the other hand, German naval expenditure can be adapted by an alteration in the tempo ... so as to render any serious increase unnecessary to meet German programme, British government will be prepared at once to pursue negotiations on the understanding that the point of naval expenditure is open to discussion, and that there is a fair prospect of settling it favourably.

Churchill in Glasgow, quoted in *The Times*, 13 February 1912:
> We should be the first to welcome any retardation or slackening in naval rivalry. We should meet any such slackening not by words but by deeds. ...

Signal from a British flagship leaving Kiel, after a visit of the fleet, as reported in *The Times*, 30 June 1914:
> Friends today, Friends in Future, Friends for Ever.

Von Tirpitz in conversation with Jagow:
> If you had only brought us a little naval agreement with England, this war would not have been necessary.
>
> MY MEMOIRS, vol. II
> *by Von Tirpitz   Hurst and Blackett, 1919*   *p.312*

---

[1] Cassel was a friend of Edward VII and George V. Ballin was head of Hamburg–Amerika Line.

7 The Outbreak of the First World War

The Sarajevo murders were committed on 28 June 1914. It was not until 4 August that Britain issued her ultimatum to Germany. In the interval, as it became clear that the murders would result in the entire Alliance System being invoked, the British Government tried desperately to preserve peace. Once it was certain that Grey's attempts at mediation would not this time succeed, the deep division in public opinion over the question of Britain's possible entry into the war reflected the split within the Cabinet itself.

Why did Britain declare war on Germany on 4 August 1914?

Why did the Government finally decide to join France and Russia? Because of Sarajevo? Because hostility towards Germany was so intense that a conflict was widely expected? Because Britain was bound morally, if not on paper, to the Entente?

On 2 August Germany launched her attack on France across Belgian territory. This concerned Britain deeply, first as one of the 1839 Guarantors of Belgian neutrality, but also because British security was directly affected by political changes in the European States facing her across the Channel. Was the German invasion of Belgium the decisive factor in the Government's decision of 4 August?

Did Britain's reaction to the news of the Sarajevo murders suggest that she would be drawn into a war resulting from them?

In common with most other European papers, *The Times*, 29 June 1914, concentrated on the results of the assassination within the Hapsburg Empire:

> The disappearance of so vigorous, albeit incalculable a personality from Austro-Hungarian public life cannot fail profoundly to affect the destinies of the monarchy.

> At the British Foreign Office it was generally thought that the assassination of Francis Ferdinand on 28 June would have few major repercussions.
>
> FOREIGN OFFICE AND FOREIGN POLICY, 1898–1914
> *by Z. Steiner   Cambridge, 1969*   *p.155*

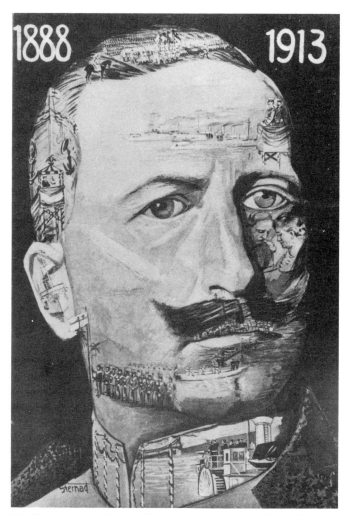

This German postcard (1913) illustrates the emphasis placed by the Kaiser on military and naval power.

The *Manchester Guardian*, 18 June 1914:

> Austria has declared war on Servia. It was expected, and the invasion of Servia is just as likely to improve as to worsen the relations between the Great Powers ... Let the war be a duel for honour's sake not a thrashing or a murderous assault.

At the same time there was clearly awareness of the wider implications.
The Times, 1 August 1914:

> In Great Britain precautionary measures are being pushed forward with great rapidity. The British Government is, however, continuing its efforts to save European peace and is in constant communication with the principal European Capitals.

The Times, 1 August 1914:

> Great Britain has no interest in the claims of either Austria-Hungary, or Servia, but as the leading power in a democratic Europe ... she is deeply concerned with Austria-Hungary's disregard of European interests and of the rudimentary principles of civilized international intercourse.

Eyre Crowe, 24 July 1914:

> France and Russia consider that these charges are the pretext, and the bigger cause of the Triple Alliance versus the Triple Entente is definitely engaged. ... Our interests are tied up with those of France and Russia in this struggle, which is not for the possession of Serbia, but one between Germany aiming at political dictatorship in Europe, and the powers who desire to retain individual freedom.
>
> *D.D.F. 3rd Series Vol. X No. 101*

Letter from Guy Fleetwood Wilson to *The Times*, 1 August 1914:

> Sir.
>
> I write as a man in the street. Doubtless I am an abnormally dense one, because I cannot for the life of me see why on earth this country should be dragged into war.
>
> How can it possibly matter to us whether or not a strong Servia is a menace to Austria or whether Russia feels compelled to intervene and Germany to follow suit? It is not worth the life of one single British Grenadier. And what earthly advantage can it be to France to follow suit?
>
> In any case, however, our interests have become too worldwide to admit of their being jeopardized in a European quarrel which only very very remotely concerns us.

Had relations between Germany and Great Britain deteriorated to the point where any pretext would serve as an excuse for war between them? Despite the continuing fear of German naval expansion, and the failure of Haldane's mission, there is evidence of an improvement in relations prior to Sarajevo.

During the Balkan Wars, Anglo-German co-operation had, not once but repeatedly, taken the sting out of a dangerous crisis.
BRITAIN IN EUROPE, 1789–1914
by R. Seton-Watson   Cambridge, 1937   *p.641*

Grey proposing a new formula to ease the arms race, 14 March 1912: England will make no attack upon Germany and pursue no aggressive policy towards her.
B.D. No. 537

Bethmann Hollweg to Goschen, 10 January 1913:
I can assure you that if it had not been for England and Germany, Europe would be in a state of war at this moment.
B.D. IX (II) No. 484

Benckendorff. Despatch of February 1912:
Sir Edward Grey has always denied both in public and in conversation with me, that he aimed at isolating Germany. He has said repeatedly to me that any attempt to break up the Triple Alliance would be a mistake. In his view the isolation of Germany would mean an actual danger to peace.

Haldane visited Germany in 1912, to try to end naval rivalry:
[Haldane] twice told Metternich he was anxious for better relations, and spoke with sympathetic understanding of Germany's desire for expansion. He even spoke of the possibility of a quadruple grouping of Britain, France, Russia and Germany. In June he went so far as to suggest to Grey that he should do as the Germans wished and induce France to be more friendly to Germany.
THE END OF ISOLATION
by G. Monger   Nelson, 1963   *p.299*

Nicolson to Hardinge, 29 October 1913:
There is no doubt that the party in favour of intimate relations with Germany has increased and strengthened of late in this country. I am afraid, personally, supposing a collision did occur between France and Germany, that we should waver as to what course we should pursue until it was too late.
LORD CARNOCK
by H. Nicolson   Constable, 1930   *p.402*

Lloyd George in the House of Commons, 23 July 1914:
Our relations are very much better than they were a few years ago. The two great Empires begin to realise they can co-operate for

70

DAILY DISPATCH: MONDAY; JULY 11; 1910.

SOFT ADVICE v. HARD FACTS.

The FANATIC : "Now, if you only got rid of that heavy burden from your shoulders, you'd be able to ascend to heights you never even dreamt of."

The TURTLE : "Yes, WITH SOMEBODY ELSE'S CLAWS IN MY BACK !"

common ends, and that the points of co-operation are greater and more numerous and more important than the points of possible controversy.

Hansard Parliamentary Debates 5th Series Vol. IXV 1914 Col. 727

Pro-German feeling was expressed in the Press. The *Manchester Guardian*, 8 July 1914:

I can see no signs of the Anti-German sentiment so common in London a few years ago.

The Economist, 1 August 1914:

It is very noticeable that there were many cries of 'Hoch England' as the crowds that demonstrated in Berlin last Saturday passed the British Embassy. It is deplorable that at such a moment Mr Churchill should have given sensational orders to the Fleet, as if forsooth, whatever happens, any British Government was entitled to plunge this nation into the horrors of war in a quarrel which is no more of our making than would be a quarrel between Argentina and Brazil . . . .

New Statesman, 1 August 1914:

Formerly when the centre of gravity in Europe was further west than it is, there was more virtue in a Franco-German balance . . . France's stagnancy in population seems removing her inevitably from the lists, while the vast development of Germany, and the even more gigantic strides of Russia make the question of balance in future a question between these two Powers. It is one in which our policy in weighing the weaker scale must almost certainly lead us tomorrow, if not today, to place ourselves on Germany's side. The tendency is already manifest in the Anglo-German rapprochement during and since the Balkan wars. But a war now would interrupt it before it is ripe.

Letter from group of leading scholars, from the *Manchester Guardian*, 1 August 1914:

We regard Germany as a nation leading the way in Arts and Science . . . a war upon her in the interest of Servia and Russia will be a sin against civilization.

A serious consideration for the British Cabinet in July 1914 was the pressure put on them by the two Powers with whom they had Ententes, France and Russia. Were the moral obligations Britain owed to them, together with the Naval Agreements reached with France, enough to bring her into the war? On this, more than any other consideration, opinion was divided.

By 1907, Grey's commitment to the French was complete. His constantly reiterated claims of full freedom of action were mere exercises in public relations.

THE CRISIS OF IMPERIALISM
by R. Shannon   Hart-Davis MacGibbon, 1974   *p.417*

C.P. Scott to Grey:

. . . this Country was so intimately involved (in the 3rd Moroccan Crisis) that had war broken out between France and Germany, we must in all probability have been a party to it' wrote C.P. Scott to Grey, protesting at the Government's policy, and he went on to urge the Foreign Secretary that the Entente 'is not to be understood as an alliance, and that it leaves us perfectly free to enter into similar negotiations with other European powers and notably with Germany'.

Grey. Memo of 24 September, 1912:

The question of whether we went to war would depend on how the war came about. No British Government could go to war unless

backed by public opinion. Public opinion would not support any aggressive war for a 'revanche'. .... If, however, Germany was led by her great, I might say, unprecedented strength to attempt to crush France, I did not think we should stand by and look on but should do all we could to prevent France from being crushed.
TWENTY-FIVE YEARS, vol. I
by Lord Grey   Hodder, 1925   *p.297*

Isvolsky to Sazanov[1], 5 December 1912:
Since the beginning of the present (1912) crisis, Monsieur Poincaré has continually been urging the London Cabinet to engage in confidential discussions in order to gain a clear knowledge of the attitude which Britain proposes to take up in the event of a general European conflict. As to this Britain has hitherto entered no engagement. ... On the other hand, every conceivable possibility has been examined by the French and British general staffs, and not only has this gone on without intermission but the existing naval and military agreements have quite recently been considerably extended, so that the Anglo-French military convention is now worked out in every detail like the Franco-Russian, and equally exhaustive.

Sazanov to Benckendorff, 19 February 1914:
The peace of the world will be secure only when the Triple Entente ... is transformed into a defensive alliance without secret clauses. Then the danger of a German hegemony will be finally ended.

Beckendorff in reply:
If Grey could, he would do it tomorrow.
Mezhdunarodnye Otnosheniya   3rd Series

Churchill commenting on the Anglo-French Military Conversation:
The moral claims which France could make up on Great Britain, if attacked by Germany, whatever we stipulated to the contrary, were enormously extended.
THE WORLD CRISIS, 1911–1914
by Winston Churchill   Butterworth, 1923   *p.32*

The Times Leader, 1 August 1914:
For us, whatever may befall, this cannot be a war of national hatred. We have nothing to avenge and nothing to acquire. In this vital issue we can only be guided by two considerations – the duty we owe to our friends and the instinct of self preservation . . .. The armies now marshalling against our friends challenge in reality our security not less than theirs.

---

[1] Isvolsky was Russian Ambassador in Paris. Sazanov was Russian Foreign Minister.

Grey to the House of Commons, 3 August 1914:

The French Fleet is now in the Mediterranean, and the Northern and Western coasts of France are absolutely undefended . . . . The French Fleet is in the Mediterranean, and has for some years been concentrated there because of the feeling of confidence and friendship which has existed between the two countries. My own feeling is that if a foreign fleet engaged in a war which France had not sought, and in which she had not been the aggressor, came down the English Channel and bombarded and battered the undefended coasts of France, we could not stand aside and see this going on practically within sight of our eyes, with our arms folded, looking on dispassionately, doing nothing! I believe that that would be the feeling of this Country.

Hansard Parliamentary Debates 5th Series Vol. IXV 1914 Col. 1810–27

Earl Loreburn, writing in 1919:

We were brought into the war because Mr Asquith and Sir Edward Grey . . . had placed us in such a position toward France and therefore also toward Russia, that they found they could not refuse to take up arms on her behalf when it came to the issue. . . . We went to war unprepared in a Russian quarrel because we were tied to France in the dark.

It is just as easy to find evidence on the other side.

R. Shannon comments on the situation in 1911:

In some very unpleasant Cabinet recriminations Grey was supported only by Asquith, Haldane, Lloyd George and Churchill. They were obliged to agree to a strict formula laying down that no military or naval arrangements entered into with other countries could directly or indirectly commit Britain to military or naval intervention and that such arrangements should henceforth not be entered into without the previous approval of the Cabinet.

THE CRISIS OF IMPERIALISM

by R. Shannon   Hart-Davis MacGibbon, 1974   *p.432*

Grey to Bertie, 9 January 1913:

War would be very inconvenient. I do not think we could take part in it and intervene on the Russian side.

B.D. IX No. 537

In April 1914 Grey visited Paris with George V, and 'felt he could afford to parade British freedom of manoeuvre and refuse to promise British support for Russia against Germany'.

74

BY ATTEMPTING TO BE BOTH—
ONE MAY FAIL TO BE EITHER.

THE DUCK: "Ven I try to be king of der water, der fish won't let me; und ven I claim to be king of der land, blest if old Chanticleer don't object!"

In answer to the new German Army Bill, the French Government proposes to spend a sum of over £23,000,000 in increasing and perfecting the military resources of the Republic.

Grey to Bertie, 1 May 1914:

> If there were a really aggressive and menacing attack made by Germany upon France, it was possible that public feeling in Great Britain would justify the Government in helping France. But it was not likely that Germany would make an aggressive and menacing attack upon Russia; and even if she did, people in Great Britain would be inclined to say that, though Germany might have successes at first, Russia's resources were so great, that in the long run, Germany would be exhausted without our helping Russia.
> *B.D. X(II) No. 541*

Grey to Cambon, 1 August 1914:
> France must take her own decision at this moment without reckoning on any assistance we are not now in a position to promise.
>
> *F/O. 800/426*

To which Nicolson commented:
> You will render us a byword among nations.

Nicolson to Hardinge, 5 September 1914:
> You will no doubt have read the White Paper, but I may tell you quite privately that ... the Cabinet were not prepared to stand by France.
>
> *F/O. 800/375*

Comments in the Press. The *Manchester Guardian* Leader, 1 August 1914:
> Evidence grows that public opinion is becoming shocked and alarmed at the thought that this country could be dragged into the horrors of a general European war ... the British Government is, on the testimony of the Prime Minister and the Foreign Secretary entirely free from any obligation to fight on the side of Russia or France or any European Power. .... The Foreign Secretary (in the Commons Debate) continued 'The Prime Minister then replied that if war arose between the European Powers there were no unpublished agreements which would restrict or hamper the freedom of the Government or of Parliament to decide whether or not Britain should participate in war ...'.

Henry Nuttall, M.P., in a Leader to the *Manchester Guardian*, 1 August 1914:
> The crime we should commit in taking part in the war which the Government has stated we are under no obligation to do ... should impel any humane man and woman to exercise all the influence of which he or she is capable to secure our neutrality and non intervention. We could then employ our influence, with hands unstained with human blood, to work for the restoration of peace, and modify the horrors of what we call war, but which is nothing less than wholesale murder. If we are in it, we shall add to the conflagration, which may bring about a catastrophe to ourselves without any parallel in our history.

Grey to the House of Commons, 3 August 1914:
> I think it is obvious ... that we do not construe anything which has previously taken place in our diplomatic relations with other Powers in this matter as restricting the freedom of the Government to decide what attitude they should take now, or restrict the

Map showing the Franco-German Frontier and Belgium.

freedom of the House of Commons to decide what their attitude should be. ... I can say this with the most absolute confidence – no Government and no country has less desire to be involved in war over a dispute with Austria and Servia than the Government and country of France. They are involved in it because of their obligation of honour under a definite alliance with Russia. Well, it is only fair to say to the House that that obligation of honour cannot apply in the same way to us. We are not parties in the Franco-Russian Alliance. We do not even know the terms of that Alliance. So far I have, I think, faithfully and completely cleared the ground with regard to the question of obligation.

Hansard Parliamentary Debates 5th Series Vol. LXV 1914 Col. 1810–27

Goschen to Grey, 8 August 1914:

He [Bethmann Hollweg] said that the step taken by His Majesty's Government [the Ultimatum] was terrible to a degree; just for a word – 'neutrality', a word which in wartime had so often been disregarded – just for a scrap of paper Great Britain was going to make war on a kindred nation who desired nothing than to be friends with her ....

DIPLOMATIC DOCUMENTS OF THE EUROPEAN WAR
H.M.S.O., 1915   *p.111*

Was the German Chancellor's analysis of Britain's actions in August 1914 correct? Concern over Belgium is a recurring theme in military talks from the beginning of the century.

Memo to General Staff, 29 September 1905:

1. In the event of a Franco-German war, would there be a strong inducement for either of the belligerents to violate the neutrality of Belgium?
3. In what time from the order to mobilize could the British Army Corps be disembarked in Belgium?
C.D. Records Cab. 4/1

[British interests] were now more than ever opposed to the violation of Belgian territory. ... [Because] the German point of view has changed, the need for preparation for active measures in defence of Belgian neutrality would be much greater than in 1870.
MY WORKING LIFE
by Lord Sydenham   Murray, n.d.   *p.153*

... the Cabinet decided on 2nd August to treat German violation of Belgian neutrality as a casus belli. This was the decisive turning point .... Belgium enabled a majority of the Cabinet to judge the

'Balance of Power' issue. Had the Germans reverted to their pre-Schlieffen strategic plan and turned first against the Russians in full co-operation with the Austrians and held back the French in Alsace Lorraine, it is extremely doubtful if Britain could have gone to war.

THE CRISIS OF IMPERIALISM
by R. Shannon   Hart-Davis MacGibbon, 1974   *p.459*

Grey to Goschen, 4 August 1914:
The King of the Belgians has made an appeal to His Majesty the King for diplomatic intervention on behalf of Belgium in the following terms:– 'Remembering the numerous proofs of your Majesty's friendship . . . I make a supreme appeal to the diplomatic intervention of your Majesty's Government to safeguard the integrity of Belgium'.

His Majesty's Government are also informed that the German Government have delivered to the Belgian Government a note proposing friendly neutrality entailing free passage through Belgian territory . . . . We also understand that Belgium has categorically refused this as a flagrant violation of the law of nations.

His Majesty's Government are bound to protest against the violation of a treaty to which Germany is a party in common with themselves, and must request an assurance that the demand made upon Belgium will not be proceeded with and that her neutrality will be respected by Germany. You should ask for an immediate reply.

DIPLOMATIC DOCUMENTS OF THE EUROPEAN WAR
H.M.S.O., 1915   *p.107*

Grey to the House of Commons, 3 August 1914:
I shall have to put before the House at some length what is our position in regard to Belgium. The governing factor is the Treaty of 1839. . . . It is one of those Treaties which are founded, not only on consideration for Belgium . . . but in the interests of those who guarantee the neutrality of Belgium. The honour and interests are, at least, as strong today as in 1870 . . . .
Diplomatic intervention took place last week on our part. What can diplomatic intervention do now? We have great and vital interests in the independence . . . of Belgium . . . . If her independence goes, the independence of Holland will follow. I ask the House from the point of view of British interests, to consider what may be at stake . . . . If in a crisis like this, we run away from these obligations of honour and interest as regards the Belgian Treaty, I doubt whether, whatever material force we might have in the end,

it would be of very much value in face of the respect we should have lost.

Hansard Parliamentary Debates 5th Series Vol. LXV 1914 Col. 1810–27

Grey to Villiers (English Minister at Brussels) 4 August 1914:

You should inform Belgian Government that if pressure is applied to them by Germany to induce them to depart from neutrality, Her Majesty's Government expect that they will resist by any means in their power, and that His Majesty's Government will support them in offering such resistance, and that His Majesty's Government in this event are prepared to join Russia and France, if desired, in offering ... at once common action for the purpose of resisting use of force by Germany against them ....

DIPLOMATIC DOCUMENTS OF THE EUROPEAN WAR
H.M.S.O., 1915   *p.108*

Grey to Goschen, 4 August 1914:

We are also informed that Belgian territory has been violated at Gemmenich. In these circumstances, and in view of the fact that Germany declined to give the same assurance respecting Belgium as France gave last week ... we must repeat that request, and ask that a satisfactory reply to it and to my telegram of this morning be received here by 12 o'clock tonight. If not, you are instructed to ask for your passports, and to say that His Majesty's Government feel bound to take all steps in their power to uphold the neutrality of Belgium and the observance of a treaty to which Germany is as much a party as ourselves.

DIPLOMATIC DOCUMENTS OF THE EUROPEAN WAR
H.M.S.O., 1915   *p.109*

Declaration of War, 5 August 1914:

The following statement was issued from the Foreign Office at 12.15 this morning:

Owing to the summary rejection by the German Government of the request made by His Majesty's Government for assurances that the neutrality of Belgium will be respected ... His Majesty's Government have declared to the German Government that a state of war exists between Great Britain and Germany ....

We have refused quietly to stand by and witness the perpetration of the direst crime that ever stained the pages of history.

A contemporary assessment from the *Spectator*, December 1914:

If Germany had tried to invade France by the direct route instead of by way of Belgium, we should still have been under a profound obligation to help France and Russia. It is useless to tell us that we were free to act as we pleased. All our dealings with France had committed us to her cause as plainly as if we had entered into a binding alliance with her. And what is true of our understanding with France is true in a scarcely less degree of our understanding with Russia.

A.J.P. Taylor's assessment:

The Powers of the Triple Entente all entered the war to defend themselves. . . . Great Britain had a moral obligation to stand by France and a rather stronger one to defend her Channel Coast. But she went to war for the sake of Belgium and would have done so, even if there had been no Anglo-French Entente.

THE STRUGGLE FOR MASTERY IN EUROPE, 1848–1918

by A.J.P. Taylor   Oxford, 1954   *p.527*

Further Reading

R. Blake *Disraeli* (EYRE & SPOTTISWOODE, 1966)

A. Bullock *Illustrated History of the Twentieth Century* (THAMES & HUDSON, 1971)

K. Bourne *The Foreign Policy of Victorian England* (CLARENDON, 1970)

G. Cecil *Life of Robert, Lord Salisbury* (HODDER, 1921–32)

W. Churchill *World Crisis* (BUTTERWORTH, 1923)

Erskine Childers *The Riddle of the Sands* (NELSON, 1903)

H. Gollwitzer *Europe in the Age of Imperialism* (THAMES & HUDSON, 1969)

J. Grenville *Lord Salisbury and Foreign Policy* (ATHLONE PRESS, 1964)

C. Howard *Splendid Isolation* (MACMILLAN, 1967)

Hurd & Castle *German Sea Power* (MURRAY, 1913)

P. Kennedy *Tirpitz, England and the Second Law of 1900* (MILITARGESCHICHTLICHE MITTEILUNGEN, 1970)

A. Kennedy *Salisbury, 1830–1914* (MURRAY, 1953)

P. Knaplund *Great Britain's Imperial Policy* (ALLEN & UNWIN, 1928)

Kapton & Derry *Europe, 1815–1914* (MURRAY, 1969)

W. Langer *The Diplomacy of Imperialism* (KNOPF, NEW YORK, 1951)

W. Langer *European Alliances and Alignments, 1871–1890* (KNOPF, NEW YORK, 1950)

C. Lowe *The Reluctant Imperialists* (ROUTLEDGE & KEGAN PAUL, 1967)

H. Lutz *Lord Grey and the World War* (ALLEN & UNWIN, 1928)

A. Marder *Fear Good and Dread Nought* (CAPE, 1952)

A. Maurois *A History of France* (CAPE, 1949)

G. Monger *The End of Isolation* (NELSON, 1963)

Monypenny & Buckle *The Life of Disraeli* (MURRAY, 1910–20)

J. Morley *The Life of William Ewart Gladstone* (MACMILLAN, 1903)

Newton (Lord) *Lord Lansdowne – a Biography* (MACMILLAN, 1929)

H. Nicolson *Lord Carnock* (CONSTABLE, 1930)

I. Nish *The Anglo-Japanese Alliance* (ATHLONE PRESS, 1966)

P. Padfield *The Great Naval Race* (HART-DAVIS MACGIBBON, 1935)

R. Seton-Watson   *Disraeli, Gladstone and the Eastern Question*
(MACMILLAN, 1936)
R. Seton-Watson   *Britain in Europe, 1789–1914*   (CAMBRIDGE, 1937)
R. Shannon   *The Crisis of Imperialism*   (HART-DAVIS MACGIBBON,
1974)
Z. Steiner   *The Foreign Office and Foreign Policy*   (CAMBRIDGE, 1938)
Temperley & Penson   *The Foundations of British Foreign Policy*
(CAMBRIDGE, 1938)
E. Woodward   *Great Britain and the German Navy*   (OXFORD, 1935)
Zetland (Marquis of)   *Lord Cromer*   (HODDER, 1932)

Autobiographies
Grey (Lord)   *Twenty-five Years*   (HODDER, 1925)
Vansittart (Lord)   *The Mist Procession*   (HUTCHINSON, 1958)
Von Tirpitz   *My Memoirs*   (HURST & BLACKETT, 1919)

Letters
Sir F. Ponsonby (ed.)   *Letters of the Empress Frederick*
(MACMILLAN, 1928)
Buckle (ed.)   *Letters of Queen Victoria*   (MURRAY, 1930)
Ramm (ed.)   *Political Correspondence of Mr Gladstone and Lord
Granville*   (OXFORD, 1962)
Balfour (ed.)   *Personal and Literary Letters of 1st Earl of
Lytton*   (LONGMAN, 1906)

Private Papers
Balfour MSS   Bertie MSS   Campbell-Bannerman MSS
Hardinge MSS   Lascelles MSS   Lord Rendel MSS
Eckardstein *Lebenserinnerung*   Von Tirpitz *Politische Dokumente*

Document Collections
British Documents on the Origins of the War (B.D.)   1927
Diplomatic Documents on the Origins of the War   (Gooch & Temper-
ley, 1926–36)
Diplomatic Documents of the European War   (H.M.S.O., 1915)
Gladstone's Political Speeches in Scotland   (ed. by A. Ramm, OXFORD,
1962)
Public Record Office – *Admiralty, Cabinet Papers, Foreign Office
Papers*
Die Grosse Politik der Europaischen Kabinette (G.P.)   1922–26
Mezhdunarodnye Otnosheniya   1930

Papers & Journals

Daily Chronicle
Daily News
Manchester Guardian
The People
The Sun

The Times
The Economist
The New Statesman
The Quarterly Review
The Spectator

Hansard Parliamentary Debates

Acknowledgments
and Sources

page 10   Advertisement for Pears Soap from ILLUSTRATED LONDON NEWS, 1887.

page 29   Russian postcard. *British Museum.*

page 30   French cartoon from L'ASSIETTE AU BEURRE, 1904

page 35   Illustration from PICTURES OF LITTLE ENGLANDERS by R.A. Forster, 1876. *British Museum.*

page 35   Alberich, guardian of the treasure of the Nibelungen, from a production of Wagner's *The Ring of the Nibelungen*, Bayreuth 1876.

page 38   Boer War cartoon. *Radio Times Hulton Picture Library.*

page 39   Boer War cartoon. *Mary Evans Picture Library.*

page 47   Cartoon from L'ASSIETTE AU BEURRE, 1903.

page 56   Postcard. *Altonaer Museum, Hamburg.*

page 60   Front page of MANCHESTER GUARDIAN, Monday 3 August 1914. *British Newspaper Library.*

page 63   Cartoon from DAILY DISPATCH, Thursday 14 March 1912. *British Newspaper Library.*

page 64   Cartoon from DAILY DISPATCH, Friday 17 May 1912. *British Newspaper Library.*

page 67   Postcard. *Altonaer Museum, Hamburg.*

page 70   Cartoon from DAILY DISPATCH, Monday 11 July 1910. *British Newspaper Library*

page 74   Cartoon from DAILY DISPATCH, Wednesday 19 February 1913. *British Newspaper Library*